18 BEST EVER PREM STARS!

4 KAKA!

42 TOP MOMENTS OF EURO 2008!

50 FERNANDO TORRES!

81 SUPER STADIUMS!

CHECK OUT THE WEBSITE WWW.MATCHMAG.CO.UK

10 THINGS WE LOVE ABOUT...

KAKA!

MATCH CAN'T GET ENOUGH OF THE AC MILAN & BRAZIL LEGEND!

1
He can score loads of amazing goals with both feet!

2
He won the FIFA World Player Of The Year award in 2007!

3
The Milan star's got a totally awesome goal celebration!

4
He scored ten goals when Milan won the 2007 Champo League!

5
He's married to mega-hot babe Caroline Celico!

6

The Samba ace netted an amazing double at Old Trafford in 2007!

ANDERSON'S HAIR!

What's it trying to do?

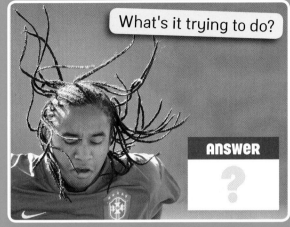

answer
?

A) Escape from the United star's head!
B) Poke his opponents in the eye!
C) Turn into a giant spider!

7

He's been the best player in Serie A for the last five years!

ACM 1899

8

Kaka's one of the greatest Brazilian players of all time!

LITTLE & LARGE!

Check out the smallest and tallest players in the Premier League!

6'6"
6'0"
5'6"
5'0"

I DIDN'T KNOW BABIES COULD TALK!

I DIDN'T KNOW GIANTS WERE REAL!

WRIGHT-PHILLIPS
5'5"

CROUCH
6'7"

GUESS WHO?

No. 1

9

He does loads of modelling for top fashion label Armani!

10

He's still only 26, so he's gonna be around for ages!

ANSWER: Ronaldinho, AC Milan.

HEY! WHERE'S MY MASK?

POW!

DROGBA WOULD BE... BATMAN!

Just like the Dark Knight, Chelsea goal machine Drogba upsets loads of people! But you know you'd love him if he was on your team!

roes!

KABOOM!

I'M GONNA SMASH YOU UP!

TERRY WOULD BE... IRON MAN!

England captain JT's a total machine! The ace centre-back is miles stronger than anyone else and can take loads of punishment!

★★★ **MAGIC** ★★★
MAN. UNITED!

Man. United have won the Premier League title a record ten times! MATCH looks back at the Red Devils' amazing run of success!

★★★ **1992-93** ★★★

★★★ **1993-94** ★★★

★★★ **1995-96** ★★★

★★★ **1996-97** ★★★

★★★ **1998-99** ★★★

★★★ **1999-00** ★★★

★★★ **2000-01** ★★★

★★★ **2002-03** ★★★

★★★ **2006-07** ★★★

★★★ **2007-08** ★★★

A IS FOR... AC MILAN! The Serie A giants have won the famous trophy seven times!

B IS FOR... BERNABEU! Real Madrid's wicked stadium will stage the final in 2010!

C IS FOR... CLARENCE SEEDORF! The Holland legend has won the trophy with AC Milan, Real Madrid and Ajax!

D IS FOR... DEPORTIVO! The La Liga club got stuffed 8-3 by Monaco in 2003! How bad is that?

I IS FOR... ITALY! The 2009 final will be played in Italy's capital city, Rome!

J IS FOR... JUVENTUS! You've got to feel sorry for Juve – they've lost in five finals!

K IS FOR... KAKA! The AC Milan hero bagged ten goals in the 2006-07 competition!

CHAMPIONS

O IS FOR... OLE! Ole Gunnar Solskjaer scored the winner as Man. United beat Bayern Munich in the 1999 final!

Q IS FOR... QUALIFIERS! Loads of teams have to get through qualification rounds just to reach the group stages!

S IS FOR... SPONSORS! The Champo League has tons of mega-rich sponsors! They bring in loads of extra cash for UEFA!

P IS FOR... PENALTIES! The 2003, 2005 and 2008 finals were all won by the dreaded penalty shoot-out!

R IS FOR... RAUL! Real Madrid's ace striker has bagged the most goals in the tournament's history!

T IS FOR... TROPHY! We love the Champions League trophy! It's the coolest cup in footy by miles!

E IS FOR... ENGLAND!
The awesome trophy has been lifted by English clubs 11 times!

G IS FOR... GROUP STAGES!
Every team has to finish first or second in the groups to qualify for the knockout stages!

H IS FOR... HEROES!
Normal players can become footy heroes in the Champo League, just like Deco in 2004!

F IS FOR... FINAL TEARS!
Arsenal, Liverpool and Chelsea have all lost in the Champions League final!

L IS FOR... LIVERPOOL!
The Reds have the best Champo League record in England – they've won it five times!

M IS FOR... MALDINI!
The AC Milan legend has played the most games in Champo League history!

N IS FOR... NOTT'M FOREST!
The Championship club have won the mega trophy twice – in 1979 and 1980!

LEAGUE! A TO Z

U IS FOR... UEFA!
The guys at UEFA make this tournament happen! For that reason, they're legends!

W IS FOR... WENGER!
The Arsenal manager is a footy legend, but he's never won the Champo League!

Y IS FOR... YAWNING!
That's what the whole of Europe was doing during the 2003 final – AC Milan 0-0 Juventus!

V IS FOR... VAN BASTEN!
The Ajax manager's lethal finishing helped AC Milan win the trophy in 1989 and 1990!

X IS FOR... XABI ALONSO!
The classy midfielder scored Liverpool's third goal when they beat AC Milan in the 2005 final!

Z IS FOR... ZIDANE!
He scored the greatest Champions League goal of all time in the 2002 final!

KEANO'S MAD CAREER!

LIVERPOOL STAR ROBBIE KEANE HAS PLAYED FOR TONS OF TOP CLUBS!

I COULDN'T HANDLE ALL THE PASTA!

HELLO GOALS!

WOLVES
1997-1999
The ace striker kicked off his career at Wolves and scored two goals on his debut!

COVENTRY
1999-2000
Keano moved to Coventry for £6 million and scored 12 Prem goals in his only season there!

INTER MILAN
2000-2001
Inter Milan bought Robbie for £13 million but he never really settled in Italy!

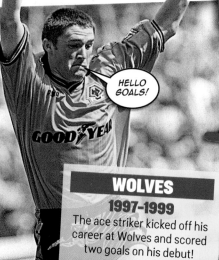

LEEDS
2001-2002
Keano didn't play much at the San Siro, so he moved back to the Prem for £12 million!

GET YOUR CASH OUT, LEEDS!

TOTTENHAM
2002-2008
He moved on to Spurs for £7 million and netted over 100 goals at White Hart Lane!

I LOVE HOLDING UP WHITE KITS!

"I'M GONNA BE AN ANFIELD LEGEND!"

LIVERPOOL

2008-PRESENT

Keano then joined the club he supported as a boy last summer for £20.3 million!

KEANO'S TOTAL TRANSFER FEES £53.8 MILLION!

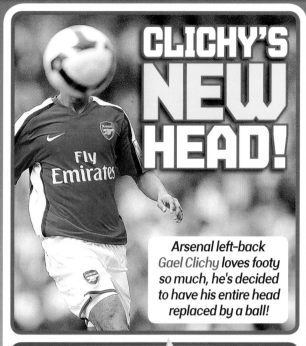

CLICHY'S NEW HEAD!

Arsenal left-back *Gael Clichy* loves footy so much, he's decided to have his entire head replaced by a ball!

WHO'S THIS OLD DUDE?

CHECK IT!

KANYE SCOLARI!

Check out Chelsea boss Phil Scolari dropping his hood down! He reckons he's a top rapper like Kanye West!

GUESS WHO?

No.2

ANSWER: Luca Toni, Bayern Munich.

BEST OF 2008...
CAUGHT ON CAMERA!

MATCH PICKS OUT THE FUNNIEST FOOTY SNAPS OF 2008!

If Ghana had played more footy and done less dancing, they might have won the Africa Cup Of Nations!

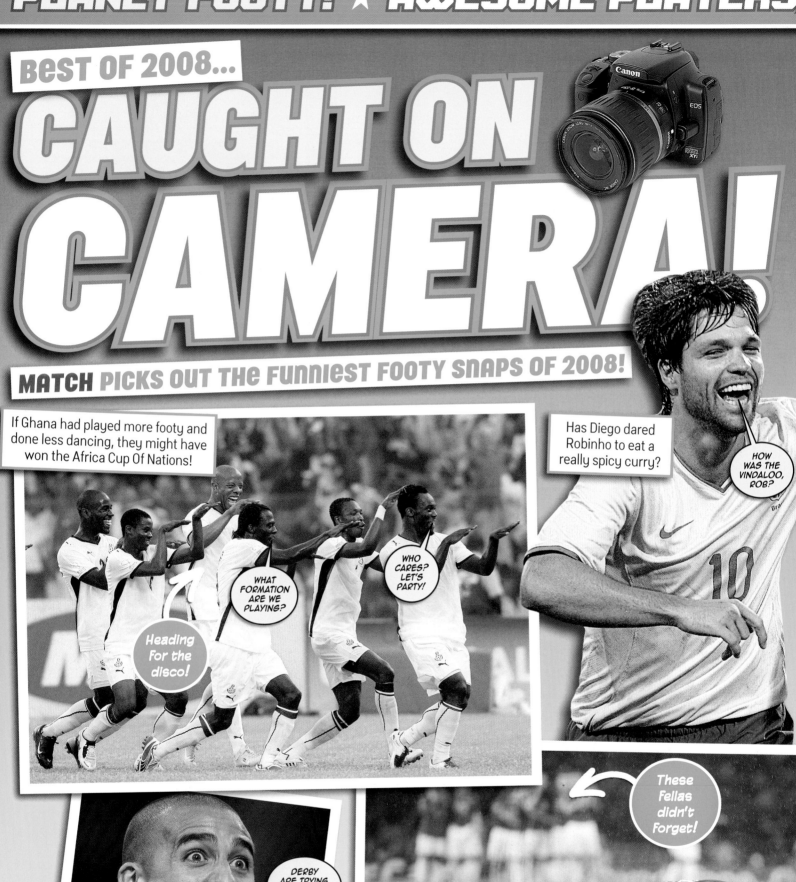

Heading for the disco!

WHAT FORMATION ARE WE PLAYING?

WHO CARES? LET'S PARTY!

Has Diego dared Robinho to eat a really spicy curry?

HOW WAS THE VINDALOO, ROB?

DERBY ARE TRYING TO SIGN ME? AARRGGH!

David Trezeguet has just been given some bad news!

These Fellas didn't Forget!

I'LL HAVE TO WATCH THE QUEEN'S SPEECH NOW!

John Terry forgot to record the Soccer AM Christmas Special!

Looks like Jens Lehmann needs a few cooking tips!

On Fire!

I THINK THE PIES ARE DONE, LADS!

Never on Fire!

PEPE'S GOT...

THE X FACTOR

I SING LIKE AN ANGEL!

Looks like Liverpool keeper Pepe Reina wants to be a pop star!

CALL THE FIRE BRIGADE, PAL!

Ronaldinho isn't too happy with the weather in Italy!

WHAT'S ALL THIS PINK SNOW, MATCH?

CHEEKY AGUERO!

GIANINNA MARADONA

DIEGO MARADONA

SERGIO AGUERO

Awesome Atletico Madrid goal machine Sergio Aguero is dating Argentina footy legend Diego Maradona's daughter!

So that's why Liverpool gaffer Rafa Benitez sold John Arne Riise to Roma!

I'M GONNA GET IN TROUBLE FOR THIS!

Air shot!

GUESS WHO?

No. 3

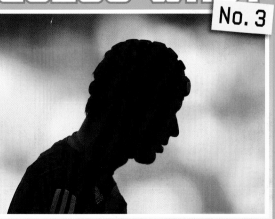

ANSWER: Petr Cech, Chelsea.

THE NEXT BIG THING!

ARSENAL's JACK WILSHERE is one of the hottest young talents in world footy! MATCH gives you all the big info on the 16-year-old with the world at his feet!

FACTPACK!

CLUB: Arsenal

AGE: 16

POSITION: Attacking midfielder

TRANSFER VALUE: £5 million

TOP SKILL: Awesome vision!

Check out matchmag.co.uk for some ace Wilshere videos!

YOUNG GUNNER!
Arsenal's latest wonderkid was born on January 1, 1992. That's just three months before Ryan Giggs made his Man. United debut!

GETTING STARTED!
The classy midfield playmaker joined Arsenal's academy in October 2001 – he was only nine years old at the time!

AWARD WINNER!
Wilshere scored two goals and was named Player Of The Tournament as Arsenal's Under-16s won the Atalanta Cup in Italy last summer!

FAVE POSITION!
Jack's favourite position is just behind the strikers, but he also played on the left and right wings for the first team in pre-season!

RESERVES DEBUT!
The tricky young star made his debut for Arsenal's reserves against Reading last season, and popped up to score the winning goal!

INTERNET STAR!
The left-footed hero first shot to fame on a Youtube video after curling home an amazing goal against West Ham's reserves! Check it out!

TOP STRENGTHS!
Jack's an awesome dribbler, has a wicked footy brain, loads of tricks and a powerful shot! He's gonna be a top Prem player!

BIG MATCHES!
Wilshere has already played for the Arsenal first team against top Euro sides! He faced Real Madrid, Juventus and Stuttgart last summer!

FIRST GOALS!
The attacking ace hit his first two goals for Arsenal in a 10-2 win against Austrian team Burgenland in a pre-season friendly!

ENGLAND MAN!
Jack has already played for England's Under-16s and Under-17s! Loads of people reckon he's gonna become a massive star for The Three Lions!

> "IT'S EASY TO FORGET HOW OLD JACK IS WHEN YOU SEE HIM PLAY!"
> ARSENE WENGER

Andrei ARSHAVIN

FREE-

8:14 PORTSMOUTH 1 32:36
0 MINS

MANU

MAN. UNITED	2
PORTSMOUTH	0

Date: January 30

Stadium: Old Trafford

Competition: Premier League

What happened? Just three minutes after netting the game's opening goal, Cristiano Ronaldo scored one of the 2007-08 season's most memorable goals! He crashed a 30-yard free-kick into the top corner, leaving Pompey keeper David James rooted to his line!

KICK KING!

THE 50 GREATEST PREM PLAYERS EVER!

MATCH COUNTS DOWN THE HOTTEST PLAYERS IN PREMIER LEAGUE HISTORY!

50 STAN COLLYMORE

POSITION: Striker
COUNTRY: England

PREM HISTORY: Bradford (2000-01), Leicester (2000), Aston Villa (1997-2000), Liverpool (1995-97), Nottingham Forest (1993-95)

After making his name with Nottingham Forest, electric striker Stan Collymore joined Liverpool in 1995 for a British record £8.5 million! Stan never quite lived up to his massive potential, but he scored some of the Prem's greatest goals!

49 STUART PEARCE

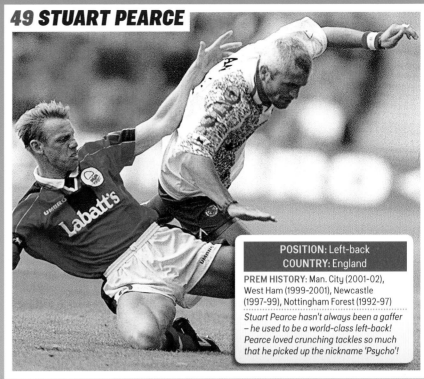

POSITION: Left-back
COUNTRY: England

PREM HISTORY: Man. City (2001-02), West Ham (1999-2001), Newcastle (1997-99), Nottingham Forest (1992-97)

Stuart Pearce hasn't always been a gaffer – he used to be a world-class left-back! Pearce loved crunching tackles so much that he picked up the nickname 'Psycho'!

48 SHAY GIVEN

POSITION: Goalkeeper
COUNTRY: Republic Of Ireland

PREM HISTORY: Newcastle (1997-present), Blackburn (1994-97)

Given's been playing in the Prem for over 14 years, and you can count the number of mistakes he's ever made on one hand! Newcastle paid just £1.5 million for him in 1997 and he's been their No.1 ever since!

47 PETER BEARDSLEY

POSITION: Forward
COUNTRY: England

PREM HISTORY: Bolton (1997-98), Newcastle (1993-97), Everton (1992-93)

Tricky forward Peter Beardsley was 30 when he made his Prem debut, but he went on to bag loads of goals for Everton and Newcastle! His footy brain rocked!

46 SAMI HYYPIA

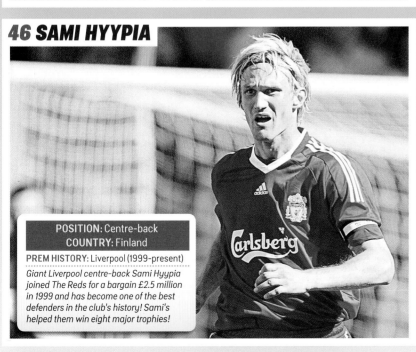

POSITION: Centre-back
COUNTRY: Finland

PREM HISTORY: Liverpool (1999-present)

Giant Liverpool centre-back Sami Hyypia joined The Reds for a bargain £2.5 million in 1999 and has become one of the best defenders in the club's history! Sami's helped them win eight major trophies!

45 FERNANDO TORRES

POSITION: Striker
COUNTRY: Spain

PREM HISTORY: Liverpool (2007-present)

El Nino has only played one full season in the Prem, but it was totally awesome! The Liverpool striker broke the record for the most goals in a debut season from a foreign player by hitting the net 24 times!

44 ANDREI KANCHELSKIS

POSITION: Winger
COUNTRY: Russia

PREM HISTORY: Southampton (2002), Man. City (2001), Everton (1995-96), Man. United (1992-95)

Kanchelskis is one of the fastest players the Prem has ever seen! Andrei loved burning down the wing for Man. United, and helped them win two Prem titles before signing for Everton in 1995!

43 CESC FABREGAS

POSITION: Midfielder
COUNTRY: Spain

PREM HISTORY: Arsenal (2004-present)

Fab made his Prem debut in 2004-05 and has been Arsenal's top player ever since! He scored seven Prem goals and set up 19 before bagging the PFA Young Player Of The Year award last season!

42 DAVID SEAMAN

POSITION: Goalkeeper
COUNTRY: England

PREM HISTORY: Man. City (2003-04), Arsenal (1992-2003)

Arsenal legend Seaman played over 400 league games for The Gunners and won two Premier League titles with the North London club! He also picked up 75 England caps during an amazing career!

41 PETR CECH

POSITION: Goalkeeper
COUNTRY: Czech Republic

PREM HISTORY: Chelsea (2004-present)

Not many footy fans had heard of Cech before Chelsea signed him for £7 million in 2004, but now he's one of the world's top keepers! He's twice been named the best goalkeeper in Europe by UEFA!

40 GARY McALLISTER

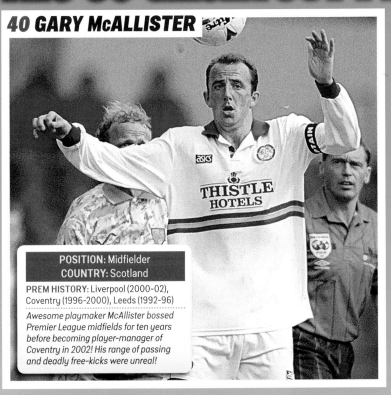

POSITION: Midfielder
COUNTRY: Scotland

PREM HISTORY: Liverpool (2000-02), Coventry (1996-2000), Leeds (1992-96)

Awesome playmaker McAllister bossed Premier League midfields for ten years before becoming player-manager of Coventry in 2002! His range of passing and deadly free-kicks were unreal!

39 FREDDIE LJUNGBERG

POSITION: Winger
COUNTRY: Sweden

PREM HISTORY: West Ham (2007-08), Arsenal (1998-2007)

Swedish ace Ljungberg netted 46 Prem goals for The Gunners in nine seasons, and even helped them win the league and FA Cup double in 2001-02 before moving to Upton Park in 2007!

38 DAVID GINOLA

POSITION: Winger
COUNTRY: France

PREM HISTORY: Everton (2002), Aston Villa (2000-02), Tottenham (1997-2000), Newcastle (1995-97)

Ginola was a magical winger who could change a game with a classy dribble or lethal long-shot! He played his best footy for Newcastle and Tottenham, winning the League Cup with Spurs in 1999!

37 MARK VIDUKA

POSITION: Striker
COUNTRY: Australia

PREM HISTORY: Newcastle (2007-present), Middlesbrough (2004-07), Leeds (2000-04)

Powerful hitman Viduka scored 59 goals in 130 games for Leeds, including four in one game against Liverpool in 2000! He was a hero during his three years at Boro and still has a few good years left in him!

36 DAVID JAMES

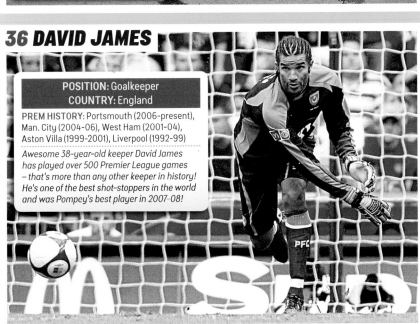

POSITION: Goalkeeper
COUNTRY: England

PREM HISTORY: Portsmouth (2006-present), Man. City (2004-06), West Ham (2001-04), Aston Villa (1999-2001), Liverpool (1992-99)

Awesome 38-year-old keeper David James has played over 500 Premier League games – that's more than any other keeper in history! He's one of the best shot-stoppers in the world and was Pompey's best player in 2007-08!

35 STEVE McMANAMAN

POSITION: Winger
COUNTRY: England

PREM HISTORY: Man. City (2003-05), Liverpool (1992-99)

Macca played over 270 Prem games for Liverpool and was a big favourite with Reds fans for his deadly dribbling and wonder goals! He left England for Real Madrid in 1999, but came back to finish his career with Man. City!

34 ROBERT PIRES

POSITION: Winger
COUNTRY: France

PREM HISTORY: Arsenal (2000-06)

Pires joined Arsenal for £6 million in 2000 as a replacement for Dutch winger Marc Overmars! The classy wideman's incredible vision and lethal finishing helped The Gunners pick up two Premier League titles!

33 PAOLO DI CANIO

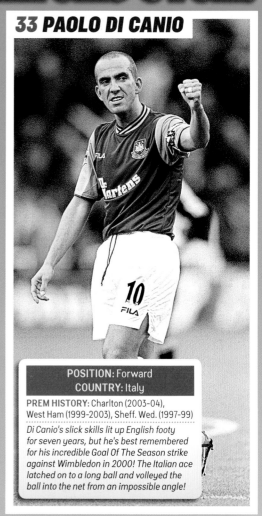

POSITION: Forward
COUNTRY: Italy

PREM HISTORY: Charlton (2003-04), West Ham (1999-2003), Sheff. Wed. (1997-99)

Di Canio's slick skills lit up English footy for seven years, but he's best remembered for his incredible Goal Of The Season strike against Wimbledon in 2000! The Italian ace latched on to a long ball and volleyed the ball into the net from an impossible angle!

32 DIDIER DROGBA

POSITION: Striker
COUNTRY: Ivory Coast

PREM HISTORY: Chelsea (2004-present)

The Drog joined Chelsea for £23.8 million in July 2004 and hit 16 goals in each of his first two seasons with The Blues! The powerhouse striker then bagged 20 Prem goals in 2006-07 and is still one of the greatest hitmen on the planet!

31 JAMIE CARRAGHER

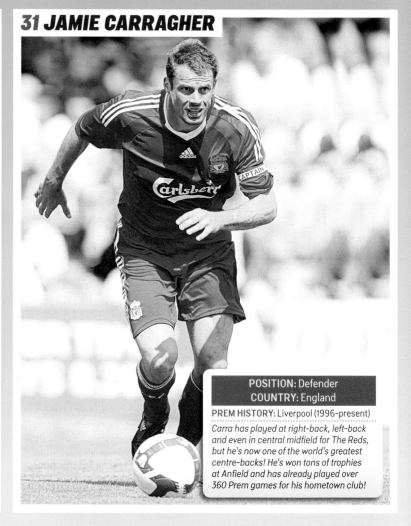

POSITION: Defender
COUNTRY: England

PREM HISTORY: Liverpool (1996-present)

Carra has played at right-back, left-back and even in central midfield for The Reds, but he's now one of the world's greatest centre-backs! He's won tons of trophies at Anfield and has already played over 360 Prem games for his hometown club!

30 TEDDY SHERINGHAM

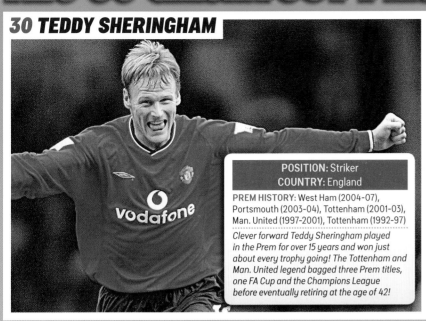

POSITION: Striker
COUNTRY: England

PREM HISTORY: West Ham (2004-07), Portsmouth (2003-04), Tottenham (2001-03), Man. United (1997-2001), Tottenham (1992-97)

Clever forward Teddy Sheringham played in the Prem for over 15 years and won just about every trophy going! The Tottenham and Man. United legend bagged three Prem titles, one FA Cup and the Champions League before eventually retiring at the age of 42!

28 DWIGHT YORKE

POSITION: Striker
COUNTRY: Trinidad & Tobago

PREM HISTORY: Sunderland (2006-present), Birmingham (2004-05), Blackburn (2002-04), Man. United (1998-2002), Aston Villa (1992-98)

Yorkie scored tons of awesome goals for Villa before moving to Man. United for £12.6 million in 1998! He formed a deadly strike partnership with Andy Cole at Old Trafford and has netted a mega 123 Prem goals in his career!

29 SOL CAMPBELL

POSITION: Centre-back
COUNTRY: England

PREM HISTORY: Portsmouth (2006-present), Arsenal (2001-06), Tottenham (1992-2001)

Big Sol spent nine years with Spurs before moving to North London rivals Arsenal on a free transfer in 2001. The powerful England centre-back won five major trophies with The Gunners and is still doing a wicked job for Harry Redknapp's Portsmouth side!

27 TONY ADAMS

POSITION: Centre-back
COUNTRY: England

PREM HISTORY: Arsenal (1992-2002)

Giant centre-back Tony Adams spent his entire career with Arsenal and is one of the best captains in the club's history! He was quality at reading the game, pure dynamite in the air and led The Gunners to two Prem titles before retiring in 2002!

26 JOHN TERRY

POSITION: Centre-back
COUNTRY: England

PREM HISTORY: Chelsea (1998-present)

Chelsea legend JT came through the youth system at Stamford Bridge before making his first-team debut back in 1998. The England skipper won the PFA Player Of The Year Award in 2005 and still has plenty of great years ahead of him!

25 PETER SCHMEICHEL

POSITION: Goalkeeper
COUNTRY: Denmark

PREM HISTORY: Man. City (2002-03), Aston Villa (2001-02), Man. United (1992-99)

Schmeichel is one of the all-time great goalkeepers! The 'Great Dane' won five Premier League titles and three FA Cups with United, and also captained them to glory in the 1999 Champions League final!

24 JIMMY FLOYD HASSELBAINK

POSITION: Striker
COUNTRY: Holland

PREM HISTORY: Charlton (2006-07), Middlesbrough (2004-06), Chelsea (2000-04), Leeds (1997-99)

The powerhouse striker was unstoppable during his spells with Leeds and Chelsea! Jimmy could score great goals with both feet, was quality in the air and bagged an amazing 128 Premier League goals!

23 RUUD VAN NISTELROOY

POSITION: Striker
COUNTRY: Holland

PREM HISTORY: Man. United (2001-06)

Ruud's a pure goal machine! He was the Prem's top scorer in 2002-03 and bagged an amazing 95 league goals in just five years at Old Trafford! That's an average of 19 league goals a season!

21 WAYNE ROONEY

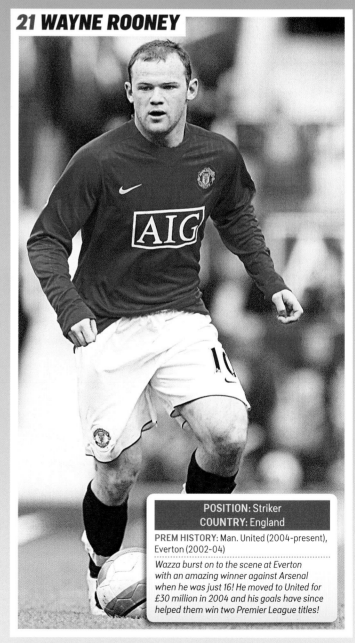

POSITION: Striker
COUNTRY: England

PREM HISTORY: Man. United (2004-present), Everton (2002-04)

Wazza burst on to the scene at Everton with an amazing winner against Arsenal when he was just 16! He moved to United for £30 million in 2004 and his goals have since helped them win two Premier League titles!

22 LES FERDINAND

POSITION: Striker
COUNTRY: England

PREM HISTORY: Bolton (2004-05), Leicester (2003-04), West Ham (2002-03), Tottenham (1997-2003), Newcastle (1995-97), QPR (1992-95)

'Sir Les' is one of the greatest headers of a ball in English footy history! He was a Loftus Road legend during his time with QPR and hit 25 league goals as Newcastle came so close to winning the title in 1996!

20 IAN WRIGHT

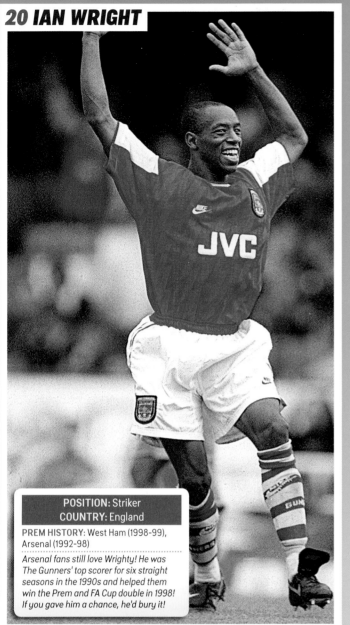

POSITION: Striker
COUNTRY: England

PREM HISTORY: West Ham (1998-99), Arsenal (1992-98)

Arsenal fans still love Wrighty! He was The Gunners' top scorer for six straight seasons in the 1990s and helped them win the Prem and FA Cup double in 1998! If you gave him a chance, he'd bury it!

19 PAUL SCHOLES

POSITION: Midfielder
COUNTRY: England

PREM HISTORY: Man. United (1994-present)

Scholes is one of the best playmakers in Premier League history! His wicked vision, precise passing and awesome goals have helped The Red Devils win eight league titles during his time with the club!

18 GARY SPEED

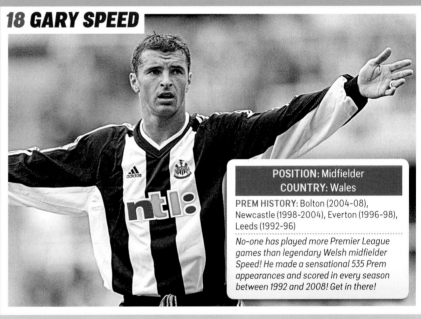

POSITION: Midfielder
COUNTRY: Wales

PREM HISTORY: Bolton (2004-08), Newcastle (1998-2004), Everton (1996-98), Leeds (1992-96)

No-one has played more Premier League games than legendary Welsh midfielder Speed! He made a sensational 535 Prem appearances and scored in every season between 1992 and 2008! Get in there!

17 ANDY COLE

POSITION: Striker
COUNTRY: England

PREM HISTORY: Sunderland (2007-08), Portsmouth (2006-07), Man. City (2005-06), Fulham (2004-05), Blackburn (2001-04), Man. United (1995-2001), Newcastle (1993-95)

Only the great Alan Shearer has scored more Premier League goals than Andy Cole! He hit the net an amazing 187 times in the top flight, won five league titles and is one of only two players to score five times in one game!

16 ROBBIE FOWLER

POSITION: Striker
COUNTRY: England

PREM HISTORY: Liverpool (2006-07), Man. City (2003-06), Leeds (2001-03), Liverpool (1993-2001)

Liverpool legend Fowler scored over 30 goals for three straight seasons between 1995 and 1997 and holds the record for the fastest Prem hat-trick – just four minutes and 33 seconds against Arsenal in 1994!

15 ROY KEANE

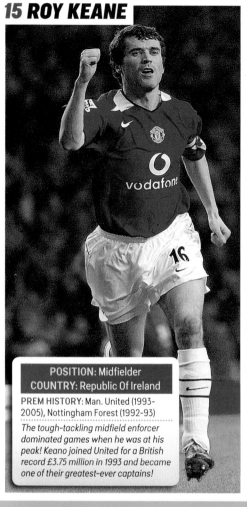

POSITION: Midfielder
COUNTRY: Republic Of Ireland

PREM HISTORY: Man. United (1993-2005), Nottingham Forest (1992-93)

The tough-tackling midfield enforcer dominated games when he was at his peak! Keano joined United for a British record £3.75 million in 1993 and became one of their greatest-ever captains!

14 MATT LE TISSIER

POSITION: Forward
COUNTRY: England

PREM HISTORY: Southampton (1992-2002)

Le Tiss is one of the most talented stars ever to play in England! He scored 101 Prem goals – and most of them were totally awesome! His mega 40-yard strike against Blackburn in 1994 was voted Goal Of The Season!

13 ERIC CANTONA

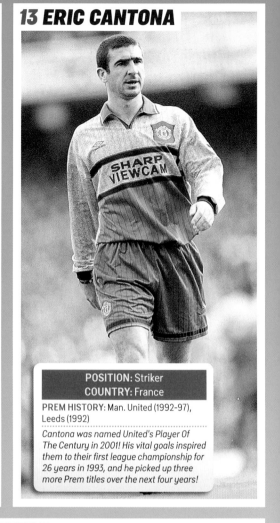

POSITION: Striker
COUNTRY: France

PREM HISTORY: Man. United (1992-97), Leeds (1992)

Cantona was named United's Player Of The Century in 2001! His vital goals inspired them to their first league championship for 26 years in 1993, and he picked up three more Prem titles over the next four years!

12 FRANK LAMPARD

POSITION: Midfielder
COUNTRY: England

PREM HISTORY: Chelsea (2001-present), West Ham (1996-2001)

Chelsea's goalscoring midfielder was born to rip up the Prem! Lamps played a record 164 straight games for Chelsea between 2001 and 2005, and his goals have helped The Blues win two titles!

11 PATRICK VIEIRA

POSITION: Midfielder
COUNTRY: France

PREM HISTORY: Arsenal (1996-2005)

The awesome box-to-box midfield machine was one of the best players in the world during his nine years with Arsenal! Vieira's unstoppable displays inspired The Gunners to three Premier League titles and four FA Cup wins!

THE 50 GREATEST PREM PLAYERS EVER!

10 CRISTIANO RONALDO

POSITION: Winger
COUNTRY: Portugal
PREM HISTORY: Man. United (2003-present)

Ronaldo took a while to settle in England, but he's been red-hot for the last two years! The wing wizard slammed in 17 Prem goals in 2006-07, then netted 31 in 2007-08 as United stormed to the title both seasons!

9 MICHAEL OWEN

POSITION: Striker
COUNTRY: England
PREM HISTORY: Newcastle (2005-present), Liverpool (1997-2004)

Owen bagged on his Prem debut for Liverpool in 1997 and hasn't stopped scoring since! The ace penalty-box predator has finished as joint top scorer twice and was named European Player Of The Year in 2001!

8 DAVID BECKHAM

POSITION: Midfielder
COUNTRY: England
PREM HISTORY: Man. United (1995-2003)

Beckham's amazing goal from inside his own half against Wimbledon in 1996 is one of the Prem's greatest moments! The free-kick expert won six Prem titles before joining Real Madrid in 2003!

7 GIANFRANCO ZOLA

POSITION: Forward
COUNTRY: Italy
PREM HISTORY: Chelsea (1996-2003)

The silky Italian forward is one of the most exciting players to pull on a Chelsea shirt! Zola scored 59 Prem goals for The Blues and was voted the club's best-ever player by their fans!

6 RIO FERDINAND

POSITION: Centre-back
COUNTRY: England
PREM HISTORY: Man. United (2002-present), Leeds (2000-02), West Ham (1996-2000)

Rio's broken the transfer record for the world's most expensive defender twice, and he's worth every penny! The stylish centre-back reads the game like a legend and is every striker's worst nightmare!

5 DENNIS BERGKAMP

POSITION: Striker
COUNTRY: Holland

PREM HISTORY: Arsenal (1995-2006)

The classy striker only ever seemed to score great goals! His sensational hat-trick against Leicester back in 1997 saw him claim first, second and third place in the September Goal Of The Month award! How good is that?

4 STEVEN GERRARD

POSITION: Midfielder
COUNTRY: England

PREM HISTORY: Liverpool (1998-present)

Liverpool's inspirational skipper has been bossing English footy for ten years! The awesome midfielder has been named in the Prem Team Of The Season six times and was PFA Player Of The Year in 2006!

3 ALAN SHEARER

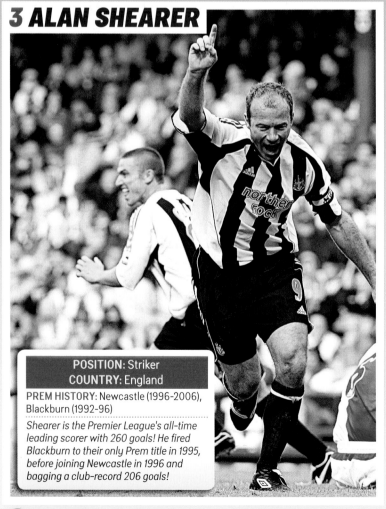

POSITION: Striker
COUNTRY: England

PREM HISTORY: Newcastle (1996-2006), Blackburn (1992-96)

Shearer is the Premier League's all-time leading scorer with 260 goals! He fired Blackburn to their only Prem title in 1995, before joining Newcastle in 1996 and bagging a club-record 206 goals!

2 THIERRY HENRY

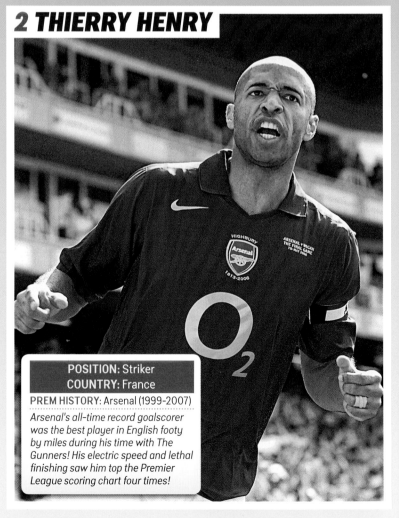

POSITION: Striker
COUNTRY: France

PREM HISTORY: Arsenal (1999-2007)

Arsenal's all-time record goalscorer was the best player in English footy by miles during his time with The Gunners! His electric speed and lethal finishing saw him top the Premier League scoring chart four times!

1 RYAN GIGGS

Bagging the PFA Young Player award in 1993!

Flying down the wing for United in 1995-96!

Giggs lifting a record tenth Prem trophy last season!

POSITION: Winger
COUNTRY: Wales

PREM HISTORY: Man. United (1992-present)

We reckon Giggsy is the best player in the history of the Premier League! The skilful left-winger has spent his whole career with United, scored in every Prem season since it started in 1992 and won a record ten titles!

WOODY

TOTTENHAM **2**

CHELSEA **1**

Date: February 24

Stadium: Wembley

Competition: Carling Cup Final

What happened? After a shocking start to the season, Juande Ramos took over from Martin Jol and led Spurs to their first major trophy since 1999! They fought back from a goal down and sealed victory when Petr Cech punched the ball on to Jonathan Woodgate's head in extra-time!

DREAM TEAM!

USE THE CLUES TO FIGURE OUT WHICH ENGLISH STARS MADE IT INTO THIS LINE-UP!

Baggies No.1 – SC!

GK
Carson

Pompey & England right-back!
RB
Johnson

Powerful Newcastle star – ST!
CB
Talyor

West Ham rock – MU!
CB
Upson

Chelsea left-back – WB!
LB
Bridge

Tottenham's £17 million hero!
RM
Bently

Bolton's midfield ace – KN!
CM
Nolan

Liverpool's awesome captain!
CM
STEVEN GERRARD

Tricky Boro wideman – SD!
LM
Downing

Arsenal's teenage speed king!
S
Wilshere
Walcot

Man. United's ex-Everton ace!
S
Saha

3 POINTS FOR EACH CORRECT ANSWER!

MY SCORE /30

PART-TIME PROS!

4 POINTS FOR EACH CORRECT ANSWER!

MY SCORE /20

WHICH AWESOME ENGLISH FOOTY HEROES ARE THINKING ABOUT CHANGING JOBS?

1. Which ancient Pompey and England ace is ready for surgery in this pic?

2. Name this giant England striker who wants to be a policeman!

3. This Chelsea superstar looks like he wants to play a game of cricket!

4. Which Three Lions legend is getting ready to join the circus?

5. Which ancient England and Man. United defender looks like a soldier here?

ANSWERS – PAGES 90-91!

Cristiano RONALDO

★ FACTFILE! ★

CLUB: Man. United

POSITION: Winger

AGE: 23

COUNTRY: Portugal

WHY HE ROCKED!

Ronaldo was the Champions League's top scorer in 2007–08 and won the PFA Players' Player Of The Year award for the second season in a row!

MATCH!
THE No.1 FOOTBALL MAGAZINE!

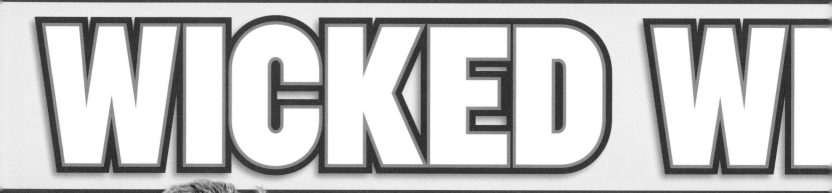

JIMMY BULLARD
FULHAM

JIMMY SAYS: "When I was playing for Wigan I filled a big dustbin up with water and leant it against one of the lads' doors in the team hotel. I knocked on the door, then ran away before he answered it. As soon as the door opened, the water poured through it and went all over his room. He was a bit annoyed!"

DARREN FLETCHER
MAN. UNITED

DARREN SAYS: "One of my old school mates told me a wind-up, so I tried it on Wes Brown. I bought some red food dye and poured it into his Predator boots. It dried overnight, but after he trained in them his feet turned bright red! They were left glowing and he couldn't get it off for days. I was really proud of that one!"

ND-UPS!

SHAY GIVEN
NEWCASTLE

SHAY SAYS: "Damien Duff does loads of wind ups! He once got one of our coaches, Terry McDermott, really badly. Duffer told him he'd dropped £20, so Terry bent down to pick it up and it flew away at the last minute. Duffer had set it up, so we all knew it was going to happen, but I still laughed for a long time!"

GARETH BARRY
ASTON VILLA

GARETH SAYS: "It was while I was playing for the England Under-21s a few years ago! One of the players got a new car, so one of the other lads decided to make him think it had been nicked by getting hold of the keys and moving it to another spot. It was well funny watching his reaction when he thought it had gone!"

JOE HART
MAN. CITY

JOE SAYS: "The best wind-up I've seen was when one of the lads put weights from the gym on the wheels of someone's car. If I remember right, it happened as payback for someone slamming the ball right in their face during training. I can't name any names, but it happened since I've been playing for Man. City!"

GARY CAHILL
BOLTON

GARY SAYS: "The best wind-up I can remember happened on England Under-21s duty. There was a live TV interview taking place outside the team hotel, so Liam Rosenior sneaked out of the back door and started dancing around in the background. It went out on Sky and we watched it on TV as it happened!"

LUKE YOUNG
ASTON VILLA

LUKE SAYS: "I was in the Spurs gym and Ben Thatcher said, 'Come here and show me what you can bench press, Youngy!' He put on way too many weights for me to lift, but I tried anyway and got trapped underneath. Then, instead of helping me, he walked around and farted in my face! I couldn't believe I fell for that!"

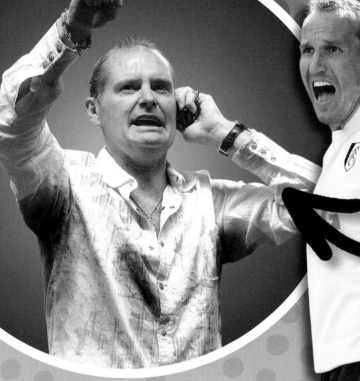

MARK SCHWARZER
FULHAM

MARK SAYS: "Paul Gascoigne was the wind-up champion when I played for Middlesbrough, and he stitched Gianluca Festa up brilliantly once! Gazza had been wearing a pair of socks for days so they really stank, then he swapped them for Festa's designer socks so he had to wear them after training! It was really funny!"

ASHLEY COLE
CHELSEA

ASHLEY SAYS: "I've seen loads of wind-ups, but nothing's made me laugh as much as something I saw in a match! Lee Dixon, the old Arsenal right-back, was on the ball in loads of space when he just fell over his feet. There was no reason for him to go over the way he did, but he went down with a bang and crashed on to the floor!"

BIG TEN!

HOW MUCH DO YOU KNOW ABOUT THE WICKED WORLD OF DUTCH FOOTY? LET'S FIND OUT!

1 Which German club did Real Madrid sign Rafael Van der Vaart From last summer?

Haburg ✓

2 Name this Holland and Ajax goal machine!

HuHer ✗

3 Which country knocked Holland out of Euro 2008?

Russia ✓

4 True or False? Clarence SeedorF has won the Champions League with two different clubs!

True ✗

5 Which Holland hero has played For Wigan, Birmingham and Chelsea?

Merlohit ✓

6 Which ex-Arsenal and Barça star is nicknamed 'Gio'?

Van Brockoosr ✓

7 Which club has never won the Dutch league title - NAC Breda, Feyenoord or Vitesse Arnhem?

Vitesse ✓

8 From which Prem club did Man. United sign Edwin Van der Sar?

Everton ✗

9 How old is classy Holland midfielder Wesley Sneijder - 24, 26 or 28 years old?

2u ✓

10 What position does Holland ace Orlando Engelaar play?

Mid ✓

5 POINTS FOR EACH CORRECT ANSWER!

MY SCORE 40 /50

ANSWERS - PAGES 90-91!

Fernando
TORRES

CHAMPO CLASSIC!

LIVERPOOL	4
ARSENAL	2

Date: April 8

Stadium: Anfield

Competition: Champions League Quarter-Final, second leg

What happened? Arsenal looked to be heading for the semi-finals when Theo Walcott beat six players and set up Emmanuel Adebayor, who tapped in with just six minutes left! But Reds skipper Steven Gerrard scored from the penalty spot before Ryan Babel wrapped up an amazing Anfield night!

BEST MOMENTS

WAS **EURO 2008** THE GREATEST FOOTY TOURNAMENT OF ALL TIME?

GREAT GOALS!

WESLEY SNEIJDER!
The Holland midfielder scored crackers against France and Italy!

MICHAEL BALLACK!
Ballack's free-kick against Austria was unstoppable!

NIHAT!
The Turkey captain's last-minute winner against the Czechs was totally amazing!

ZLATAN IBRAHIMOVIC!
Sweden's star man bagged a screamer against Greece!

RECORD BREAKERS!

HAT-TRICK HERO!
David Villa scored Spain's first ever European Championship hat-trick, and only the eighth treble in the history of the tournament!

CAP CRAZY!
Edwin Van der Sar, Lilian Thuram and Alessandro Del Piero all made their fourth appearance at the Finals, equalling the tournament record!

GOAL MACHINE!
Ruud van Nistelrooy's two goals for Holland last summer made him the joint-third highest goalscorer in Euro Championship history!

GOLDEN OLDIES!
Christian Panucci and Jan Koller, both 35, and 38-year-old Ivica Vastic became the oldest players ever to score goals at the Euros!

OF EURO 2008!

MATCH LOOKS AT THE PICK OF LAST SUMMER'S AWESOME ACTION!

CRAZY CELEBRATIONS!

MASCOT MAYHEM!
Euro 2008 mascot Flix was shown some love by Lukas Podolski after Germany beat Portugal!

THUMB-SUCKER!
Spain's Ruben de la Red pulled out this cool celebration after his rocket strike against Greece!

MAD GAFFERS!
Croatia coach Slaven Bilic went absolutely crazy on the touchline after beating Germany!

MEGA BUNDLE!
The mass pile-up after Turkey's late winner against the Czech Republic was wicked to watch!

SURPRISE STARS!

DANIJEL PRANJIC!
No-one had heard of Croatia's slick left-back before Euro 2008!

LUKAS PODOLSKI!
Podolski outshone Klose and Gomez with three goals for Germany!

PEPE!
Portugal's centre-back was solid in defence and class going forward!

ORLANDO ENGELAAR!
Holland's giant midfield anchorman dominated the middle of the park!

MEGA MATCHES!

TURKEY 3-2 CZECH REPUBLIC
Turkey's amazing comeback dumped the Czechs out!

HOLLAND 4-1 FRANCE
The Dutch hammered France in the Group Of Death!

GERMANY 3-2 PORTUGAL
Germany powered past Portugal in the quarter-finals!

RUSSIA 3-1 HOLLAND
Andrei Arshavin's Russia ripped Holland's defence to pieces!

TURKEY'S LATE SHOWS!

SWISS STUNNED!
Turkey were 1-0 down against the hosts before Semih Senturk and Arda Turan turned it all around at the end!

CZECH MATE!
Three late goals, including a cool double from Nihat, brought Turkey back from certain defeat against the Czechs!

CROATIA SHOCKER!
Semih stunned Croatia with a late extra-time equaliser, before Turkey dumped them out on penalties!

COMEBACK KIDS!

ROBIN VAN PERSIE!
The Holland striker put his injury problems behind him by bagging against France and Romania!

ANDREI ARSHAVIN!
Russia's silky playmaker was banned for the first two matches, but totally bossed things when he returned!

BASTIAN SCHWEINSTEIGER!
The Germany winger got sent off against Croatia, but bounced back with goals in the knockout stages!

SLICK SKILL!

QUARESMA'S RABONA!
Portugal ace Ricardo Quaresma busted out the most mind-blowing trick at the Euros!

SUPER SUBS!

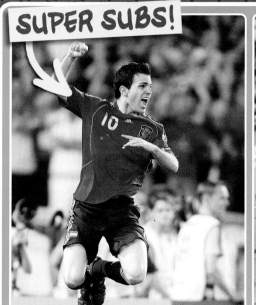

CESC FABREGAS!
Spain's midfield genius came off the bench loads
of times to make a massive impact on games!

SEMIH SENTURK!
'The Lifeguard' lived up to his weird nickname with
match-saving goals against Switzerland and Croatia!

VACLAV SVERKOS!
The Czech striker only played one game at the Euros, when he
came off the bench to score the winner against Switzerland!

MAD MOMENTS!

RUBBISH WEATHER!
Switzerland's match against Turkey turned
into a joke after this mega downpour!
The huge puddles caused total chaos!

FREI'S TEARS!
After getting injured, Switzerland's captain
just couldn't hold back the waterworks!

POTTY POGATETZ!
Emanuel Pogatetz has always been rock hard, but when the
ref gave Croatia a penalty against Austria, he totally lost it!

COOL KEEPERS!

ARTUR BORUC!
Boruc was Poland's only decent player at the Euros!
The big keeper made save after save against Austria!

GIGI BUFFON!
Buffon was top class! He kept Italy in the tournament
with an amazing penalty save against Romania!

IKER CASILLAS!
Casillas kept a clean sheet in every match during the
knockout stages and lifted the trophy as Spain captain!

CRAZY FANS!

The wicked supporters at Euro 2008 rocked for the whole tournament! Here are MATCH's favourite fans!

HOLLAND!

GERMANY!

RUSSIA!

SPAIN!

SWEDEN!

FRANCE!

ITALY!

SWITZERLAND!

TURKEY!

MEGA TACKLES!

Euro 2008 saw loads of bone-crunching challenges! Check these bad boys out!

SERGEI IGNASHEVICH!

SERGIO RAMOS!

EMRE ASIK!

CLAUDE MAKELELE!

MEHMET TOPAL!

WONDERKIDS!

ARDA TURAN!
The Turkey winger ripped up Euro 2008! His classy performances and vital late goals made him a real star!

JOAO MOUTINHO!
There was a lot of hype about Moutinho, and he didn't let himself down! He was great with Deco in Portugal's midfield!

IVAN RAKITIC!
Croatia coach Slaven Bilic loves this young winger and now we all know why! Rakitic is gonna be an awesome player!

STAR MAN – XAVI!
The ace playmaker looked like he was on a different planet! Xavi was named Player Of The Tournament!

TOP TORRES!
El Nino's winner against Germany in the final was pure quality!

COOL CESC!
Fabregas' penalty shoot-out winner against Italy put Spain through to their first major semi-final since Euro 1984!

EURO 2008 CHAMPS!
Spain were the best team in the tournament by miles! They won all their group games and didn't concede a single goal in the knockout stages!

MIDFIELD MACHINES!
Spain's wicked midfield stars totally dominated the tournament! Anchorman Marcos Senna broke up every attack that came at him, while Barcelona playmaker Andres Iniesta was a creative genius!

RECORD RUN!
Spain equalled their all-time winning streak during Euro 2008 after notching their ninth win in a row against Greece!

GOLDEN BOY!
David Villa was a goal machine! He bagged four times to finish as the tournament's leading scorer!

NAME THE TEAM!

CAN YOU REMEMBER WHICH STARS PLAYED FOR SPAIN IN THE EURO 2008 FINAL?

1 GOALKEEPER ANSWER

2 DEFENDER ANSWER

3 DEFENDER ANSWER

4 DEFENDER ANSWER

5 MIDFIELDER ANSWER

6 STRIKER ANSWER

7 WINGER ANSWER

8 WINGER INIESTA

9 MIDFIELDER ANSWER

10 MIDFIELDER ANSWER

11 DEFENDER ANSWER

4 POINTS FOR EACH CORRECT ANSWER!

MY SCORE /40

STADIUM GAME!

MATCH THESE COOL STADIUMS TO THE LA LIGA CLUBS THAT PLAY IN THEM!

2 POINTS FOR EACH CORRECT ANSWER!

MY SCORE 10 /10

THE NOU CAMP	THE MESTALLA	RIAZOR	THE BERNABEU	EL MADRIGAL
 1	 2	 3	 4	 5
A	B	C	D	E
 DEPORTIVO	 VALENCIA	 VILLARREAL	 BARCELONA	 REAL MADRID

ANSWERS - PAGES 90-91!

Dani GUIZA

★ FACTFILE! ★

CLUB: Fenerbahçe
POSITION: Striker
AGE: 28
COUNTRY: Spain

WHY HE ROCKED!

The ex-Real Mallorca goal machine was on fire in La Liga last season, bagging 27 goals to earn himself a big-money move to Fenerbahçe!

MATCH!
THE No.1 FOOTBALL MAGAZINE!

FERNANDO TORRES'

MATCH LOOKS BACK AT EL NINO'S WICKED CAREER!

SEPTEMBER 2001: RISING STAR!

Torres first shows the world what he can do by starring for Spain at the 2001 Under-17s World Championships!

OCTOBER 2002: ATLETICO ACE!

El Nino breaks into the Atletico Madrid first team and scores an impressive 12 goals in his first full season!

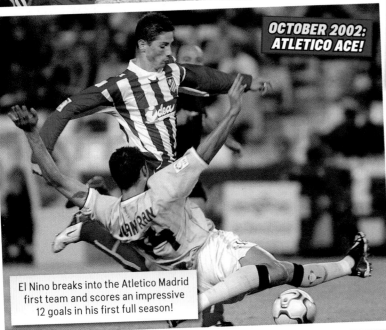

JULY 2003: PEPSI DEAL!

The wicked hitman goes big-time and stars alongside tons of massive world footy stars in a cool Pepsi advert!

Torres - Spain   Totti - Italy   R.Carlos - Brazil   Beckham - England   Ronaldinho - Brazil   Raúl - Spain   Quaresma - Portugal   Van der Vaart - Holland

SEPTEMBER 2003: BIG SPAIN DEBUT!

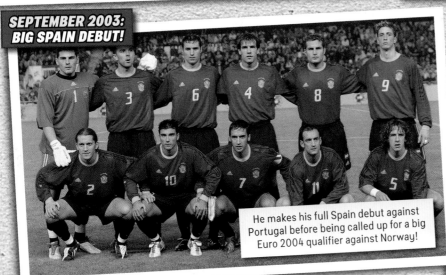

He makes his full Spain debut against Portugal before being called up for a big Euro 2004 qualifier against Norway!

JANUARY 2004: LA LIGA LEGEND!

The young striker takes La Liga by storm in 2003-04, slamming home 19 league goals as Atletico finish seventh!

SCRAPBOOK!

APRIL 2004:
FIRST SPAIN GOAL!

He opens his goal account for Spain against Italy in Genoa! The ace strike makes sure he's picked for Euro 2004!

JUNE 2004:
EURO MISERY!

Torres plays for Spain at the Euros, but it turns into a nightmare as his country crash out in the group stages!

SEPTEMBER 2004:
CAPTAIN FANTASTIC!

Aged just 19, Torres becomes Atletico's youngest-ever captain and celebrates with a classic goal against Barcelona!

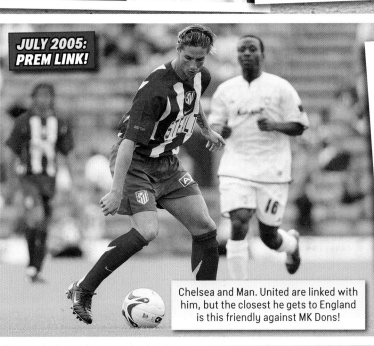

JULY 2005:
PREM LINK!

Chelsea and Man. United are linked with him, but the closest he gets to England is this friendly against MK Dons!

NOVEMBER 2005:
PLAY-OFF HERO!

Fernando hits a vital goal as Spain finally qualify for World Cup 2006 with a play-off win over Slovakia!

JUNE 2006:
WORLD CUP KING!

El Nino becomes a megastar by hitting three ace goals at World Cup 2006, but Spain lose against France in the last 16!

FEBRUARY 2007:
REAL SLAYER!

Torres celebrates a goal against city rivals Real Madrid, but confirms he'll leave Atletico at the end of the season!

FERNANDO TORRES' SCRAPBOOK!

**JULY 2007:
£26.5 MILLION MAN!**

Reds gaffer Rafa Benitez breaks Liverpool's transfer record to bring Torres to Anfield for £26.5 million!

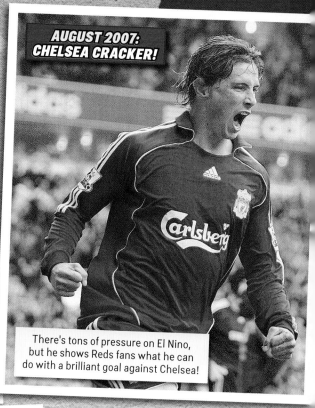

**AUGUST 2007:
CHELSEA CRACKER!**

There's tons of pressure on El Nino, but he shows Reds fans what he can do with a brilliant goal against Chelsea!

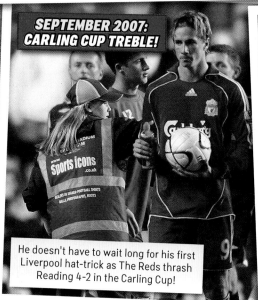

**SEPTEMBER 2007:
CARLING CUP TREBLE!**

He doesn't have to wait long for his first Liverpool hat-trick as The Reds thrash Reading 4-2 in the Carling Cup!

**OCTOBER 2007:
LATE LEVELLER!**

El Nino proves he can score important goals with an injury-time equaliser against Tottenham at Anfield!

**NOVEMBER 2007:
FIRST EURO STRIKE!**

Torres nets his first-ever goal in the Champions League with a bullet header in an easy 4-1 win over Porto at Anfield!

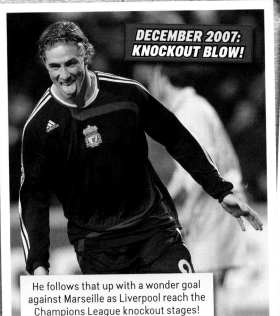

**DECEMBER 2007:
KNOCKOUT BLOW!**

He follows that up with a wonder goal against Marseille as Liverpool reach the Champions League knockout stages!

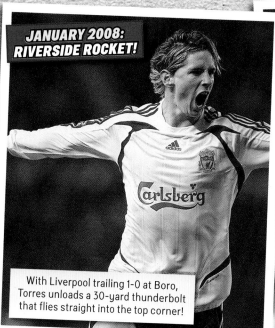

**JANUARY 2008:
RIVERSIDE ROCKET!**

With Liverpool trailing 1-0 at Boro, Torres unloads a 30-yard thunderbolt that flies straight into the top corner!

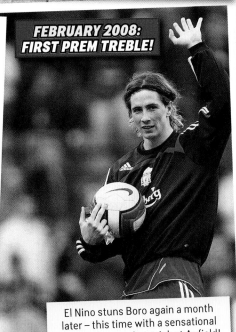

**FEBRUARY 2008:
FIRST PREM TREBLE!**

El Nino stuns Boro again a month later – this time with a sensational Premier League hat-trick at Anfield!

FEBRUARY 2008: HAMMERED!

Torres makes it two hat-tricks in two home games by grabbing three great goals in a 4-0 win over West Ham!

MARCH 2008: SAN SIRO STUNNER!

Liverpool power into the Champo League quarter-finals as Torres grabs a great winner against Inter Milan!

MARCH 2008: MERSEY MAGIC!

He scores the vital winning goal in front of the Kop as Liverpool beat local rivals Everton 1-0 at Anfield!

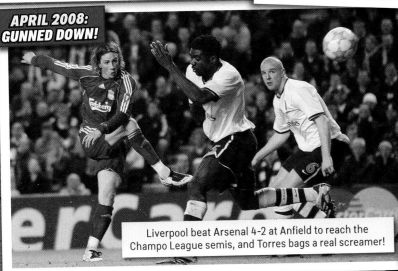

APRIL 2008: GUNNED DOWN!

Liverpool beat Arsenal 4-2 at Anfield to reach the Champo League semis, and Torres bags a real screamer!

APRIL 2008: FEELING THE BLUES!

Another El Nino goal puts Liverpool within touching distance of the final, but Chelsea fight back to win the semi!

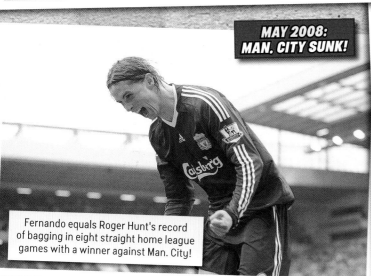

MAY 2008: MAN. CITY SUNK!

Fernando equals Roger Hunt's record of bagging in eight straight home league games with a winner against Man. City!

MAY 2008: RECORD BREAKER!

Torres bags against Spurs to become the first foreign player to score 24 goals in his first Prem season!

JUNE 2008: KING OF EUROPE!

El Nino scores a brilliant winning goal against Germany in the Euro 2008 Final as Spain claim the trophy!

ROCKIN'

RED DEVIL!

WIGAN	0
MAN. UNITED	2

Date: May 11

Stadium: The JJB

Competition: Premier League

What happened? It was an afternoon of records on the last day of the season! Sir Alex Ferguson's Man. United side picked up their tenth Premier League title and midfield legend Ryan Giggs equalled the club's appearance record of 758 games after coming off the bench to score the vital second goal!

BIG TEN!

HOW MUCH DO YOU KNOW ABOUT ITALIAN FOOTY?
TEST YOURSELF WITH THESE QUESTIONS!

1 Which Premier League club did Inter Milan's Marco Materazzi once play for?

Everton ✓

2 In which year did Gianluigi Buffon join Juventus from Parma – 1999, 2001 or 2003?

3 Which club finished fourth in Serie A last season?

Fiorontiana ✓

4 Which Italy ace top-scored for Bayern Munich in the Bundesliga last season?

Toni ✓

5 Which English League 2 club did Juventus copy their black and white shirts from?

Notts Cavenny ✓

6 How old is all-action Roma midfielder Daniele De Rossi – 25, 29 or 33 years old?

25 ✓

7 Can you name this free-kick king?

Pirlo ✓

8 Who was the only Italian to score a goal in the Prem last season?

9 Jose Mourinho is now in charge of which Italian club?

Inter ✓

10 Which Serie A club did Gianluca Zambrotta join in May 2008?

Milan ✓

5 POINTS FOR EACH CORRECT ANSWER!

MY SCORE 40/50

ANSWERS – PAGES 90-91!

Rio FERDINAND

MATCH GOES...
BACK IN

CESC FABREGAS

MULLETS LOOKED WELL COOL BACK THEN!

2004 ARSENAL

NOW ARSENAL

WES BROWN

I DID THIS FOR A DARE!

2005 MAN. UNITED

NOW MAN. UNITED

RICHARD DUNNE

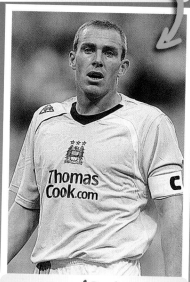

1999 EVERTON

NOW MAN. CITY

DAVID BENTLEY

I CAN'T BELIEVE I LOOK LIKE THAT NOW!

2004 NORWICH

NOW TOTTENHAM

TIME!

JOE COLE

2002
WEST HAM

NO WONDER WEST HAM SOLD ME!

NOW
CHELSEA

DJIBRIL CISSE

2006
LIVERPOOL

NOW
SUNDERLAND

JOHN CAREW

1998
VALERENGA

NOW
ASTON VILLA

DAVID BECKHAM

DON'T PRETEND YOU DON'T LOVE IT!

2001
ENGLAND

NOW
LA GALAXY

NICK BARMBY

CHECK OUT THE FLOPPY HAIR!

1993
TOTTENHAM

NOW
HULL

RICARDO CARVALHO

2003
PORTO

NOW
CHELSEA

JIMMY BULLARD

2002
PETERBOROUGH

NOW
FULHAM

JOLEON LESCOTT

2000
WOLVES

NOW
EVERTON

PAOLO MALDINI

MAN, THAT HAIR WAS WELL DODGY!

1991
AC MILAN

NOW
AC MILAN

CRAIG BELLAMY

OH NO!

2004
NEWCASTLE

NOW
WEST HAM

DAVID JAMES

I'VE ALWAYS LOOKED COOL!

2002 WEST HAM

NOW PORTSMOUTH

WILLIAM GALLAS

1999 MARSEILLE

NOW ARSENAL

PAUL SCHARNER

EVERYONE HAS PURPLE HAIR IN AUSTRIA!

2003 AUSTRIA VIENNA

NOW WIGAN

MARK VIDUKA

1999 CELTIC

NOW NEWCASTLE

FRANCESCO TOTTI

2001 ROMA

NOW ROMA

FERNANDO TORRES

I USED TO SHAVE MY OWN HEAD!

2004 SPAIN

NOW LIVERPOOL

DANNY!

Date: May 11

Stadium: Fratton Park

Competition: Premier League

What happened? It was a three-way battle for Prem survival on the final day of the 2007-08 season between Fulham, Reading and Birmingham. The Cottagers looked to be going down until Danny Murphy climbed above the Pompey defence to head home Jimmy Bullard's free-kick and keep them up!

MEGA CROSSWORD!

USE THE LETTERS IN THE GOLD BOXES TO FIGURE OUT THE 'GOALDEN' WORD!

ACROSS!

4. Age of Man. City's Jo! (6, 3)
5. Club where Kaka plays his footy! (2, 5)
7. Carlos Tevez played for this Brazilian club in 2005-06! (11)
9. Position of Tottenham's Heurelho Gomes! (6)
10. Colour of Brazil's home shorts! (4)

DOWN!

1. Boro's Brazil striker! (6, 5)
2. Position of Chelsea's Alex! (8)
3. Hull's Samba star! (8)
6. Ronaldinho's nickname! (6)
8. Awesome sports company who make Brazil's kit! (4)

Unscramble the letters in the gold boxes to work out the 'Goalden' word!

'GOALDEN' WORD

3 POINTS FOR EACH CORRECT ANSWER + 10 FOR 'GOALDEN' WORD!

MY SCORE /40

Crossword answers written in grid:
- 4 Across: TWENTY ONE
- 5 Across: AC MILAN
- 7 Across: RONNIE
- 9 Across: KEPPER
- 10 Across: BLUE
- 2 Down: DEFENDER
- 1 Down: AS ON SO A IVES
- 3 Down: GEOVANNI
- 8 Down: NIKE

SPOT THE DIFFERENCE!

CAN YOU PICK OUT THE FIVE DIFFERENCES BETWEEN THESE TWO FOOTY PICS?

2 POINTS FOR EACH CORRECT ANSWER!

MY SCORE 10 /10

Iker
CASILLAS

DID YOU KNOW?

YOU'LL LOVE THESE PREMIER LEAGUE STATS!

STAT ATTACK!

44

Hull became the 44th team to appear in the Prem when they won the Championship Play-Off Final in May 2008!

7

Seven teams have played in every Prem season! They are Arsenal, Aston Villa, Chelsea, Everton, Liverpool, Man. United and Tottenham!

133

That's the number of French players that have played in the Premier League!

Arsenal hero Patrick Vieira and former Everton striker Duncan Ferguson have both been sent off ten times in the Premier League, so don't mess!

Man. United hold the record for the Prem's biggest-ever win! Ace striker Andy Cole hit the back of the net five times as they beat Ipswich 9-0 at Old Trafford in 1995!

Ledley King scored the fastest-ever Premier League goal after just ten seconds when Tottenham drew 3-3 with Bradford in December 2000!

When Arsenal won the Prem title in 1998, they had been sixth at Christmas and were 12 points behind leaders Man. United before their wicked comeback!

Crystal Palace have been promoted to the Prem four times, but then relegated back to the Championship the next season every time! Sort it out, lads!

Birmingham's Marcus Bent has played in the Prem for seven different clubs – Crystal Palace, Blackburn, Ipswich, Leicester, Everton, Charlton and Wigan!

Sheffield United legend Brian Deane hit the first-ever Prem goal when he netted against Man. United just five minutes into the 1992-93 season!

Matthew Briggs is the youngest player to play in the Prem! The Fulham star made his debut aged just 16 years and 65 days against Boro in May 2007!

Alan Shearer has scored more Premier League goals than any other player! The England hero ripped the net an amazing 260 times for Blackburn and Newcastle!

Moritz Volz scored the 15,000th Prem goal for Fulham against Chelsea in 2006! Amazingly, it was only the second time Volzy had bagged in the Prem!

Awesome players from 89 different countries – including Bermuda, Peru, Congo, Cyprus, Montserrat and Oman – have played in the Premier League!

17

The number of Prem goals ex-Man. United hitman Ole Gunnar Solskjaer scored as a substitute!

3,039

That's how many people watched Wimbledon play Everton in 1993! It was the lowest Prem crowd ever!

164

Frank Lampard played 164 consecutive games for Chelsea between October 2001 and December 2005!

335

Ex-Sunderland defender Kenny Cunningham played a record 335 Prem games without scoring! Oh no!

CUP KING KANU!

PORTSMOUTH	1
CARDIFF	**0**

Date: May 17

Stadium: Wembley

Competition: FA Cup Final

What happened? Kanu's first-half strike proved to be the winning goal as Pompey beat Cardiff at Wembley! It was Harry Redknapp's first major trophy as a manager and the first time the South Coast club had lifted the FA Cup since 1939!

CHAMPIONS LEAGUE

CAN YOU PLAY 90 MINUTES IN THE CHAMPIONS LEAGUE FINAL AND WIN THE TROPHY BEFORE

KICK-OFF! `1 min`
Let's get the Champo League final started!
ROLL A SIX TO START!

GOAL CHANCE? `2 mins`
You get a one-on-one!
ROLL EVENS TO SCORE, ROLL ODD TO PUT IT WIDE!

ACTION! `3 mins`
You're in on goal, but the defender tracks back to tackle you!

GOAL CONCEDED? `4 mins`
Your team gets hit on the break!
ROLL EVENS TO STOP 'EM, ROLL ODD AND THEY SCORE!

ACTION! `5 mins`
You win possession in midfield and spray the ball out wide!

INJURY? `10 mins`
Your marker crashes into you!
ROLL EVENS TO GET UP, ODD FOR A CALF INJURY!

OFFSIDE! `9 mins`
You pick out your striker with a through ball, but he's offside!

YELLOW CARD! `8 mins`
You slide in late!
EVENS GETS A WARNING, ROLL ODD FOR A BOOKING!

ACTION! `7 mins`
You win the ball at the back and bring it out of defence!

GOAL CHANCE? `6 mins`
Your winger whips in a wicked cross!
ROLL EVENS TO SCORE, ROLL ODD TO MISS!

GOAL CONCEDED? `11 mins`
The opposition break forward!
ROLL EVENS TO STOP THEM, ODD MEANS THEY SCORE!

GOAL CHANCE? `12 mins`
You get on the end of a flick-on!
ROLL EVENS TO BURY IT, ROLL ODD TO MISS IT!

ACTION! `13 mins`
You win the battle with your opposition's hardman!

ACTION! `14 mins`
Your team-mate breaks from midfield and you put him through!

GOAL CHANCE? `15 mins`
You hit a 30-yard screamer!
EVENS RIPS THE NET, ODD AND IT'S SAVED!

GOAL CONCEDED? `20 mins`
Your defence gets sliced open!
EVENS SAVES THE SHOT, ODD AND YOU CONCEDE!

YELLOW CARD! `19 mins`
You tug your opponent's shirt!
EVENS GETS A WARNING, ROLL ODD FOR A BOOKING!

ACTION! `18 mins`
You're hacked down in midfield! The ref blows for a foul!

GOAL CHANCE? `17 mins`
You win a penalty!
EVENS SCORES, ODD AND THE KEEPER SAVES IT!

ACTION! `16 mins`
You follow up a rebound, but their keeper saves!

GOAL CHANCE? `21 mins`
You get another one-on-one!
EVENS CHIPS THE KEEPER, ROLL ODD AND YOU MISS IT!

INJURY? `22 mins`
You jump for the ball!
EVENS WINS THE HEADER, ROLL ODD TO CLASH HEADS!

ACTION! `23 mins`
You fly past your marker down the left-wing!

ACTION! `24 mins`
You get closed down quickly, but bust out a flash trick!

OFFSIDE! `25 mins`
You dart in between the centre-backs, but stray offside!

ACTION! `30 mins`
You keep it simple and pass to your full-back!

INJURY? `29 mins`
You're tackled late!
EVENS SKIPS THE TACKLE, ROLL ODD AND HE HURTS YOUR ANKLE!

GOAL CHANCE? `28 mins`
You meet a corner with a header!
ROLL EVENS TO NOD HOME, ROLL ODD TO HIT THE BAR!

GOAL CONCEDED? `27 mins`
You give away a penalty!
ROLL EVENS TO SAVE IT, ROLL ODD AND IT'S A GOAL!

RED CARD! `26 mins`
You're defending on your own line!
EVENS CLEARS THE BALL, ODD AND YOU GET SENT OFF FOR HANDBALL!

ACTION! `31 mins`
You launch a pinpoint cross-field pass to your full-back!

GOAL CHANCE? `32 mins`
You hit a free-kick!
EVENS CURLS IT IN THE TOP CORNER, ROLL ODD TO HIT THE WALL!

SUBSTITUTION! `33 mins`
Time for a change!
ROLL EVENS TO ESCAPE BEING SUBBED, ROLL ODD TO BE TAKEN OFF!

ACTION! `34 mins`
You follow up a rebound, but their keeper makes a wicked save!

ACTION! `35 mins`
You fly in for a 50-50 challenge!

ACTION! `40 mins`
You dummy the ball and completely fool your opponent!

ACTION! `39 mins`
You skip past your marker, but he comes back to tackle you!

YELLOW CARD! `38 mins`
You shout at the ref!
EVENS GETS A WARNING, ROLL ODD FOR A BOOKING!

GOAL CHANCE? `37 mins`
You power a header at goal!
ROLL EVENS TO NOD HOME, ROLL ODD TO HIT THE BAR!

GOAL CONCEDED? `36 mins`
You give away a free-kick!
EVENS AND IT'S BLOCKED, ODD AND IT'S A GOAL!

ACTION! `41 mins`
Your team-mate breaks from midfield and you put him through!

OFFSIDE! `42 mins`
Your team-mate makes a run, but you delay the pass too long!

GOAL CHANCE? `43 mins`
You play a neat one-two!
ROLL EVENS TO GO ON AND SCORE, ROLL ODD TO MISS!

ACTION! `44 mins`
You fly in for a 50-50!

HALF-TIME! `45 mins`
Get a drink before starting the second half on the next page!

FINAL GAME!

YOUR MATE DOES? FIND OUT IN OUR WICKED FOOTY GAME!

RULES!

★ Find a mate, roll the dice to move and follow the instructions on each square to decide what happens next!

★ Keep track of the number of goals that are scored as you play the game!

★ If you receive two yellow cards or a red card, get injured or substituted, you must start again!

★ The winner is the player who finishes the final with the most goals! Have you got the skills to grab Champo League glory?

KICK-OFF! – 46 mins
Roll the dice to get the second-half underway!

GOAL CONCEDED? – 47 mins
The opposition are clean through!
EVENS MAKES THEM MISS, ODD AND THEY SCORE!

ACTION! – 48 mins
You make a clever run off the ball!

GOAL CHANCE? – 49 mins
You spot the keeper off his line!
EVENS CHIPS HIM, ODD PUTS IT OVER!

SUBSTITUTION! – 50 mins
Your boss makes a change!
ROLL EVENS TO STAY ON, ROLL ODD TO GO OFF!

GOAL CHANCE? – 51 mins
You fight for the ball in the air!
EVENS TO SCORE, ODD AND THE DEFENDER BEATS YOU!

GOAL CHANCE? – 52 mins
Your team-mate dummies a cross!
ROLL EVENS TO TUCK IT HOME, ODD TO FLUFF IT!

YELLOW CARD! – 53 mins
You handle the ball!
EVENS GETS AWAY WITH IT, ROLL ODD TO GET BOOKED!

OFFSIDE! – 54 mins
Your defence catches the opposition striker offside!

ACTION! – 55 mins
You get closed down quickly, but still beat your marker!

ACTION! – 56 mins
You try to bring down a long ball!

GOAL CONCEDED? – 57 mins
Their striker goes through on goal!
EVENS MAKES IT GO WIDE, ODD AND HE RIPS THE NET!

ACTION! – 58 mins
You get in on goal, but the defender tracks back to tackle you!

ACTION! – 59 mins
You play a great one-two in midfield to get past your marker!

ACTION! – 60 mins
A wicked stepover gives you space to bomb down the wing!

GOAL CHANCE? – 61 mins
A poor clearance drops to you!
EVENS VOLLEYS HOME, ODD AND YOU SHANK IT!

ACTION! – 62 mins
You win possession in midfield!

SUBSTITUTION! – 63 mins
The gaffer's making a change!
ROLL EVENS TO STAY ON, ROLL ODD TO BE HAULED OFF!

GOAL CONCEDED? – 64 mins
In comes a corner!
EVENS HEADS CLEAR, ROLL ODD AND THEIR DEFENDER SCORES!

GOAL CHANCE? – 65 mins
You dribble towards goal!
ROLL EVENS TO SCORE, ROLL ODD TO GET TACKLED!

YELLOW CARD! – 66 mins
You make a bad foul!
ROLL EVENS FOR A WARNING, ROLL ODD TO GET YOUR NAME TAKEN!

ACTION! – 67 mins
You follow up a rebound, but their keeper makes a wicked save!

ACTION! – 68 mins
You time a tackle perfectly!

ACTION! – 69 mins
You pull off a great piece of skill and the crowd goes crazy!

ACTION! – 70 mins
You collect an awesome long ball from your centre-back!

ACTION! – 71 mins
You grab possession in midfield and spray the ball wide!

GOAL CONCEDED? – 72 mins
Your defence is in trouble!
EVENS INTERCEPTS, ODD AND YOU LET IT IN!

OFFSIDE! – 73 mins
You score a tap-in from a free-kick, but you get ruled offside!

GOAL CHANCE? – 74 mins
The keeper spills a shot at your feet!
EVENS TAPS HOME, ODD MISSES THE BALL!

INJURY? – 75 mins
You go in for a 50-50!
EVENS WINS THE TACKLE, ROLL ODD TO GET HURT!

GOAL CHANCE? – 76 mins
You're clean through on goal!
ROLL EVENS TO RUN ON AND SCORE, ROLL ODD TO GET CAUGHT OFFSIDE!

ACTION! – 77 mins
You get in on goal, but the defender tracks back to tackle you!

ACTION! – 78 mins
Your ace pass puts the winger clear down the wing!

GOAL CONCEDED? – 79 mins
The opposition captain hits a wonder strike!
EVENS HITS THE BAR, ODD FINDS THE TOP CORNER!

GOAL CHANCE? – 80 mins
You reach a knock down in the area!
EVENS DRILLS IT HOME, ODD MISSES THE BALL!

INJURY? – 81 mins
You try to clear!
EVENS HEADS IT AWAY, ROLL ODD AND YOU GET ELBOWED!

ACTION! – 82 mins
You keep it simple and pass the ball back to your full-back!

GOAL CHANCE? – 83 mins
You win a corner!
ROLL EVENS TO SCORE, ROLL ODD TO MISS AT THE BACK POST!

ACTION! – 84 mins
Your midfielder wins the ball!

ACTION! – 85 mins
You fire a shot at goal, but it flies just over the bar!

SUBSTITUTION! – 86 mins
You're shattered!
ROLL EVENS TO STAY ON THE PITCH, ROLL ODD TO BE SUBBED OFF!

ACTION! – 87 mins
You make a last-ditch tackle to save your team!

YELLOW CARD! – 88 mins
You trip an opponent!
EVENS GETS A TELLING OFF, ROLL ODD FOR A BOOKING!

GOAL CONCEDED? – 89 mins
Your opponents hit you on the break!
EVENS STOPS THE ATTACK, ODD AND THEY HIT THE NET!

FINAL WHISTLE! – 90 mins
The Champions League final's finished!
DID YOU WIN THE MATCH?

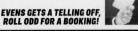

BIG TEN!

CAN YOU HANDLE THESE TEN TOUGH QUESTIONS ABOUT AWESOME ARGENTINEAN FOOTY?

1 How old is silky Boca Juniors playmaker Juan Riquelme?

2 Which club are the league champions of Argentina?

3 What is the nickname of the Argentina national team – Albicelestes or Azzurri?

Azzuri

4 In which year did Argentina last win the World Cup?

1987

5 Who scored more goals in Spain's La Liga last season – Diego Milito or Sergio Aguero?

Aguero ✓

6 Which club did Real Madrid defender Gabriel Heinze start his career with?

Man U

7 Which Argentina striker plays For Man. United?

Tevez ✓

8 Who is the captain of the Argentina national team?

9 True or False? Lionel Messi's middle name is Andres!

True ✓

10 What is the name of Boca Juniors' Famous stadium?

ANSWERS – PAGES 90-91!

David VILLA

★ FACTFILE! ★

CLUB: Valencia

POSITION: Striker

AGE: 26

COUNTRY: Spain

WHY HE ROCKED!

'The Kid' slammed home the only hat-trick of Euro 2008 and picked up the Golden Boot after finishing the tournament with four goals!

MATCH!

THE No.1 FOOTBALL MAGAZINE!

PENALTIES

4 - 4

	MANCHESTER UNITED			CHELSEA
TÉVEZ	○		○	BALLACK
CARRICK	○		○	BELLETTI
RONALDO	✕		○	LAMPARD
HARGREAVES	○		○	A.COLE
NANI	○		○	

MOSCOW MEGA MISS!

| MAN. UNITED | 1 |
| CHELSEA | 1 |

Date: May 21

Stadium: Luzhniki Stadium, Moscow

Competition: Champions League Final

What happened? After Ronaldo's weak spot-kick had been saved by Petr Cech, all Chelsea skipper John Terry had to do was score his penalty to win the Champo League! But JT slipped as he struck the ball and saw his effort clip the outside of the post! United went on to lift the famous trophy!

10

9

8

ALEX & RIGOBERT SONG
NEPHEW & UNCLE

Arsenal young gun Alex's uncle Rigobert has starred for Liverpool, West Ham and Galatasaray! They even played in the same team at the 2008 Africa Cup Of Nations!

MARK VIDUKA & LUKA MODRIC
COUSINS

We couldn't believe it when we heard these two were distant cousins! Viduka's been rocking the Prem for years, so maybe he's giving Modric some wicked tips!

PETER & KASPER SCHMEICHEL
FATHER & SON

Young Man. City shot-stopper Kasper Schmeichel has a lot to live up to, coz his dad was one of the best goalkeepers on the planet when he played for Man. United and Denmark!

7

6

IAN WRIGHT & SHAUN WRIGHT-PHILLIPS
FATHER & SON

Ian Wright is a footy legend who hit 185 goals for Arsenal! Wrighty adopted SWP when he was younger and helped him become a class winger!

5

STEVEN & ANTHONY GERRARD
COUSINS

Stevie G runs the midfield for Liverpool and England and is one of the world's top stars! Tony G started off at Everton, but he's now tearing it up with League 1 club Walsall!

SIR ALEX & DARREN FERGUSON
FATHER & SON

Sir Alex's son Darren kicked off his career at Man. United before moving on to Wolves and Wrexham! He's now in charge of Peterborough and wants to be a top gaffer!

AMILIES!

4

3

FRANK & FRANK LAMPARD
FATHER & SON

Chelsea midfielder Franky Lamps is one of the world's top players, but people forget his dad was totally awesome too! Lampard Senior played 660 games for West Ham!

GARY & PHIL NEVILLE
BROTHERS

The Neville brothers played together at Man. United for 11 years before Phil signed for Everton in 2005! They've won tons of trophies together and even played in the same England team 31 times!

2

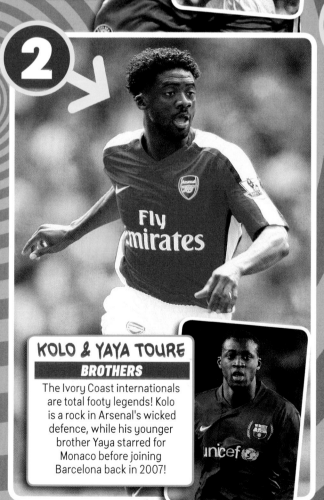

1

KOLO & YAYA TOURE
BROTHERS

The Ivory Coast internationals are total footy legends! Kolo is a rock in Arsenal's wicked defence, while his younger brother Yaya starred for Monaco before joining Barcelona back in 2007!

RIO & ANTON FERDINAND
BROTHERS

We reckon the Ferdinand boys are quality! Man. United defender Rio has won tons of trophies in his career, while Anton is gonna be a big star for new club Sunderland!

WICKED

WINDASS!

BRISTOL CITY	0
HULL	1

Date: May 24

Stadium: Wembley

Competition: Championship Play-Off Final

What happened? It was a fairytale final for Hull's 39-year-old goal king Dean Windass, who scored a stunning volley to send his hometown club into the top flight for the first time in their history! Amazingly, it was Deano's first appearance at the legendary stadium, and his third spell with The Tigers!

WICKED WORDSEARCH!

FIND THESE TEN PORTUGUESE CLUBS IN THIS MEGA GRID!

```
J X O O S F G F Y Y O L F F D S P B B A
W O Z L H E B P M X B S J B G O N E I G
W F M Y U I O C P D Z C W E J R A L T R
E I Y I U R V T K W A B T L N Y V B I I
P G P I T K F M B A Q R A E E S A M Q O
S Q A O K I P O C R O F U N C Z L C S A
S E V U J O R I J F A X E F N O T O V V
F C T V L K F A E F C G I N U J Y J C E
L Q A J S N E N M M H A A S Q Z H N O U
F Q U O E R S D Y Q I L D E E V T E X Z
Y I L B T E Y Q G E D W K S T O F K H J
N O B S I L G N I T R O P S U T X T R Q
J Q Q F M J A C I M E D A C A E I I L P
A C B F P H U A C Z K S B P Z L X T E T
M F F X N X I X W J Z S O Z T W F K V L
```

3 POINTS FOR EACH CORRECT ANSWER!

MY SCORE 30/30

STARTING POINT!

JOIN THESE PORTUGAL STARS TO THE CLUBS THEY STARTED THEIR CAREERS WITH!

4 POINTS FOR EACH CORRECT ANSWER!

MY SCORE /20

CRISTIANO RONALDO	JOSE BOSINGWA	NUNO GOMES	RICARDO CARVALHO	PEPE
 1	 2	 3	 4	 5
A	B	C	D	E
 SC FREAMUNDE	 SPORTING LISBON	 MARITIMO	BOAVISTA	 PORTO

ANSWERS - PAGES 90-91!

SUPER STADIUMS!

MATCH CHECKS OUT THE WORLD'S COOLEST FOOTY GROUNDS!

THE MARACANA ★ BRAZIL

CITY!
Rio de Janeiro

TEAMS!
Flamengo, Fluminense &
the Brazil national team

CAPACITY!
95,000

YEAR OPENED!
1950

MARACANA HERO!
Kaka

GREATEST GAME!
Santos 2-1 Vasco, Pele's
1,000th career goal, 1969

FAB FACT!
The Maracana used to be even
bigger! An amazing 199,854
people crammed in to watch
the 1950 World Cup Final!

STADE DE FRANCE ★ FRANCE

CITY!
Paris

TEAM!
France national team

CAPACITY!
80,000

YEAR OPENED!
1998

STADE DE FRANCE HERO!
Thierry Henry

GREATEST GAME!
France 3-0 Brazil,
World Cup Final, 1998

FAB FACT!
The £225 million stadium
has crazy moving stands
that can be wheeled back
to let an athletics track
fit around the pitch!

MILLENNIUM STADIUM ★ WALES

CITY!
Cardiff

TEAM!
Wales national team

CAPACITY!
76,250

YEAR OPENED!
1999

MILLENNIUM HERO!
Gareth Bale

GREATEST GAME!
Liverpool 3-3 West Ham,
FA Cup Final, 2006

FAB FACT!
The Millennium Stadium
will host at least eight
Olympic footy matches
when the Games come
to London in 2012!

OLD TRAFFORD ★ ENGLAND

CITY!
Manchester

TEAM!
Man. United

CAPACITY!
76,212

YEAR OPENED!
1910

OLD TRAFFORD HERO!
Cristiano Ronaldo

GREATEST GAME!
Man. United 4-3 Real Madrid, Champions League, 2003

FAB FACT!
There are 23 miles of heating pipes under the Old Trafford pitch that stop the ground from freezing during the winter!

SIGNAL IDUNA PARK ★ GERMANY

CITY!
Dortmund

TEAM!
Borussia Dortmund

CAPACITY!
80,708

YEAR OPENED!
1974

SIGNAL IDUNA HERO!
Alexander Frei

GREATEST GAME!
Liverpool 5-4 Alaves, UEFA Cup Final, 2001

FAB FACT!
The giant South Stand can hold 24,454 people and is the biggest terrace in Europe! Fans are still allowed to stand up at Bundesliga games!

SAN SIRO ★ ITALY

CITY!
Milan

TEAMS!
AC Milan & Inter Milan

CAPACITY!
82,955

YEAR OPENED!
1926

SAN SIRO HERO!
Ronaldinho

GREATEST GAME!
Inter Milan 1-5 Arsenal, Champions League, 2003

FAB FACT!
When it first opened in 1926, the San Siro only held 26,000 fans! But within just 14 years, the capacity was increased to a massive 150,000!

NOU CAMP ★ SPAIN

CITY!
Barcelona

TEAM!
Barcelona

CAPACITY!
98,772

YEAR OPENED!
1957

NOU CAMP HERO!
Lionel Messi

GREATEST GAME!
Man. United 2-1 Bayern Munich, Champions League Final, 1999

FAB FACT!
Barça are planning to put an extra 10,000 seats into their wicked stadium in the next five years! It's gonna cost a whopping £175 million!

THE BERNABEU ★ SPAIN

CITY!
Madrid

TEAM!
Real Madrid

CAPACITY!
80,400

YEAR OPENED!
1947

BERNABEU HERO!
Rafael Van der Vaart

GREATEST GAME!
Italy 3-1 West Germany,
World Cup Final, 1982

FAB FACT!
When Real wanted to
increase the size of their
stadium, they lowered the
pitch by two metres to
fit extra seats in!

ALLIANZ ARENA ★ GERMANY

CITY!
Munich

TEAM!
Bayern Munich & 1860 Munich

CAPACITY!
69,901

YEAR OPENED!
2005

ALLIANZ ARENA HERO!
Franck Ribery

GREATEST GAME!
France 1-0 Portugal,
World Cup Semi-final, 2006

FAB FACT!
The Allianz Arena is known as
'The Inflatable Boat' and the
outside lights up in different
colours depending on which
home team is playing!

LA BOMBONERA ★ ARGENTINA

CITY!
Buenos Aires

TEAM!
Boca Juniors

CAPACITY!
57,395

YEAR OPENED!
1940

BOMBONERA HERO!
Juan Riquelme

GREATEST GAME!
Argentina 6-3 World XI,
Diego Maradona Tribute, 2001

FAB FACT!
La Bombonera stands
for 'The Chocolate Box'!
The awesome stadium is also
known as the Estadio
Alberto J. Armando!

THE AZTECA ★ MEXICO

CITY!
Mexico City

TEAM!
Mexico national team
& Club America

CAPACITY!
105,000

YEAR OPENED!
1966

AZTECA HERO!
Giovani Dos Santos

GREATEST GAME!
Argentina 2-1 England,
World Cup Quarter-final, 1986

FAB FACT!
There's a plaque outside
the stadium to celebrate
Diego Maradona's wonder
goal against England in 1986!

WEMBLEY ★ ENGLAND

CITY!
London
TEAM!
England national team
CAPACITY!
90,000
YEAR OPENED!
2007
WEMBLEY HERO!
Wayne Rooney
GREATEST GAME!
England 1-1 Brazil, 2007
FAB FACT!
The £778 million stadium has an incredible 2,618 toilets! That's more than any other sports venue in the world!

GET A LOAD OF THESE CRAZY STADIUMS!

ESTADIO JOSE ALVALADE ★ PORTUGAL

CITY: Lisbon
TEAM: Sporting Lisbon
CAPACITY: 50,466
FAB FACT: It was built to host footy matches, but is also used for music concerts! It's got the best stadium sound quality in the world!

Gelredome ★ HOLLAND

CITY: Arnhem
TEAM: Vitesse Arnhem
CAPACITY: 32,500
FAB FACT: The Gelredome has a retractable roof and a wicked sliding pitch that rolls under one of the stands and out of the stadium!

ESTADIO AXA ★ PORTUGAL

CITY: Braga
TEAM: Sporting Braga
CAPACITY: 30,154
FAB FACT: This crazy ground has been built into a hillside, so one end of the pitch has a massive rock face instead of a stand!

BIG TEN!

PROVE YOU'RE A FRENCH FOOTY EXPERT BY TACKLING THIS BRAIN-BUSTING QUIZ!

1 Which French club did Arsenal sign Emmanuel Adebayor From in 2006?
....

2 Which team has won more Ligue 1 titles – Nantes, Monaco or St. Etienne?
St ✓

3 True or False? France legend David Trezeguet was the top scorer in Serie A last season!
False ✓

4 Which awesome French team beat Liverpool at AnField in last season's Champions League?
Marsile ✓

5 Which club did Claude Makelele leave Chelsea For at the start of the season?
PSG ✓

6 In which stadium do France play their home games?
Parc de Princes ✓

7 This wicked wonderkid was Ligue 1's top scorer in 2007-08! Who is he?
Benzema ✓

8 Which club won their seventh straight Ligue 1 title last season?
Lyon ✓

9 How many times has Barcelona striker Thierry Henry won the World Cup with France?
0 ✗

10 Which France and Bayern Munich star was injured at Euro 2008?
Ribery ✓

5 POINTS FOR EACH CORRECT ANSWER!

MY SCORE 35 /50

ANSWERS - PAGES 90-91!

Emmanuel ADEBAYOR

★ FACTFILE! ★

CLUB: Arsenal

POSITION: Striker

AGE: 24

COUNTRY: Togo

WHY HE ROCKED!

Only Cristiano Ronaldo scored more Prem goals than the ace Togo hitman in 2007-08! Ade bagged 24 times in the league for The Gunners!

MATCH!

THE No.1 FOOTBALL MAGAZINE!

MATCHY'S QUIZ!

IT'S TIME TO FIND OUT HOW MANY QUESTIONS YOU GOT RIGHT!

★ QUIZ ONE! ★
PAGE 32

DREAM TEAM!

GK – Scott Carson; RB – Glen Johnson; CB – Steven Taylor; CB – Matthew Upson; LB – Wayne Bridge; RM – David Bentley; CM – Kevin Nolan; LM – Stewart Downing; S – Theo Walcott; S – Wayne Rooney.

MY SCORE: /30

PART-TIME PROS!

1. Sol Campbell; 2. Peter Crouch; 3. Frank Lampard; 4. David Beckham; 5. Gary Neville.

MY SCORE: /20

★ QUIZ TWO! ★
PAGE 38

BIG TEN!

1. Hamburg; 2. Klaas-Jan Huntelaar; 3. Russia; 4. False – he's won it with three clubs - Ajax, Real Madrid and AC Milan; 5. Mario Melchiot; 6. Giovanni Van Bronckhorst; 7. Vitesse Arnhem; 8. Fulham; 9. 24 years old; 10. Central midfield.

MY SCORE: /50

★ QUIZ THREE! ★
PAGE 48

NAME THE TEAM!

1. Casillas; 2. Marchena; 3. Ramos; 4. Capdevila; 5. Senna; 6. Torres; 7. Silva; 9. Xavi; 10. Fabregas; 11. Puyol.

MY SCORE: /40

STADIUM GAME!

1. D; 2. B; 3. A; 4. E; 5. C.

MY SCORE: /10

★ QUIZ FOUR! ★
PAGE 56

BIG TEN!

1. Everton; 2. 2001; 3. Fiorentina; 4. Luca Toni;
5. Notts County; 6. 25 years old; 7. Andrea Pirlo;
8. Rolando Bianchi; 9. Inter Milan; 10. AC Milan.

MY SCORE: /50

★ QUIZ FIVE! ★
PAGE 64

MEGA CROSSWORD!

MY SCORE: /30

GOALDEN WORD!

Diego.

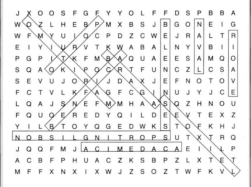

MY SCORE: /10

SPOT THE DIFFERENCE!

1. There's a different coloured stripe on ball;
2. The No.1 is missing from the Ecuador shirt;
3. Different colour on shoulder of the Ecuador shirt; 4. Brazil player's right hand is missing;
5. Number missing from Ecuador shorts.

MY SCORE: /10

★ QUIZ SIX! ★
PAGE 72

BIG TEN!

1. 30 years old; 2. River Plate; 3. Albicelestes;
4. 1986; 5. Sergio Aguero; 6. Newell's Old Boys;
7. Carlos Tevez; 8. Javier Zanetti; 9. True;
10. La Bombonera.

MY SCORE: /50

★ QUIZ SEVEN! ★
PAGE 80

WORDFIT!

MY SCORE: /30

STARTING POINT!

1. B; 2. A; 3. D; 4. E; 5. C.

MY SCORE: /20

★ QUIZ EIGHT! ★
PAGE 88

BIG TEN!

1. Monaco; 2. St. Etienne; 3. False – it was
Alessandro Del Piero; 4. Marseille; 5. PSG;
6. Stade de France; 7. Karim Benzema; 8. Lyon;
9. One; 10. Franck Ribery.

MY SCORE: /50

MY TOTAL: /400

THE POWER LEAGUE!

391-400 CHAMPIONS LEAGUE
YOU'RE A TOTAL FOOTY GENIUS!
YOU SHOULD WORK FOR MATCH!

371-390 PREMIER LEAGUE
YOUR BRAIN IS RAMMED FULL OF
MEGA FOOTY FACTS! NICE ONE!

351-370 CHAMPIONSHIP
YOU'RE ALMOST A QUIZ LEGEND, BUT
THERE'S STILL A BIT OF WORK TO DO!

301-350 LEAGUE 1
KEEP PRACTISING AND YOU WILL REACH
THE TOP ONE DAY! GOOD EFFORT!

201-300 LEAGUE 2
YOU'VE DONE ALRIGHT, BUT YOU
MISSED A COUPLE OF OPEN GOALS!

101-200 NON-LEAGUE
YOU HAD A LAUGH FILLING OUT THE ACE
QUIZZES, BUT JUST COULDN'T HACK IT!

0-100 SUNDAY LEAGUE
YOUR SCORE WAS TOTALLY RUBBISH!
YOU NEED TO RAISE YOUR GAME!

WHERE DID YOU FINISH IN MY POWER LEAGUE?

KEEP READING MATCH EVERY WEEK FOR MORE AWESOME QUIZZES!

MATCH!

THE No.1 FOR FOOTY IN 2009!

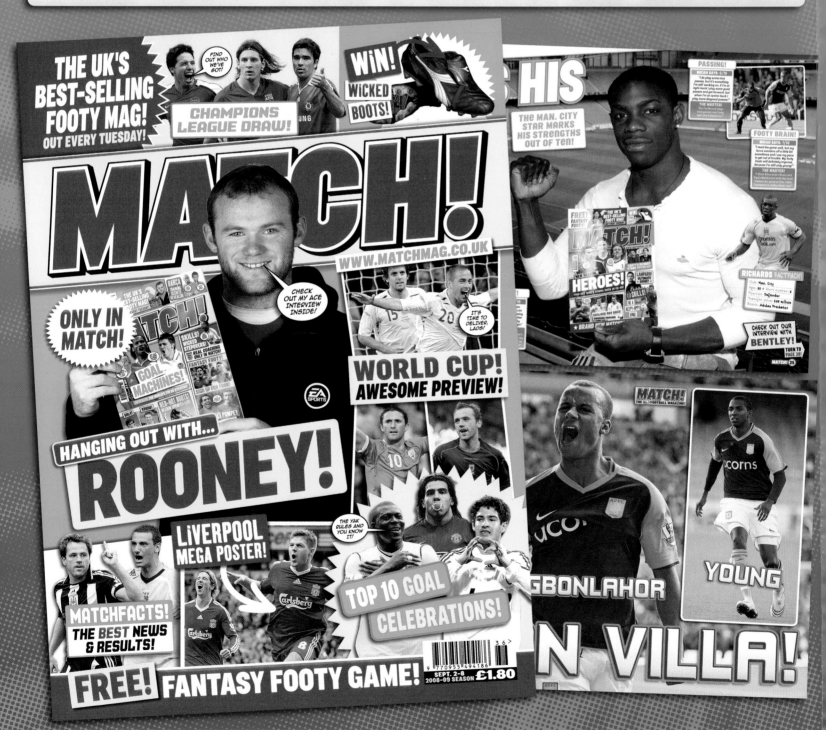

THE UK'S BEST-SELLING FOOTY MAG! OUT EVERY TUESDAY!

FIND OUT WHO WE'VE GOT!

CHAMPIONS LEAGUE DRAW!

WIN! WICKED BOOTS!

HIS

THE MAN. CITY STAR MARKS HIS STRENGTHS OUT OF TEN!

PASSING!

RICHARDS FACTPACK!

CHECK OUT OUR INTERVIEW WITH BENTLEY! TURN TO PAGE 20!

MATCH!

ONLY IN MATCH!

CHECK OUT MY ACE INTERVIEW INSIDE!

WWW.MATCHMAG.CO.UK

IT'S TIME TO DELIVER, LADS!

WORLD CUP! AWESOME PREVIEW!

HANGING OUT WITH... ROONEY!

LIVERPOOL MEGA POSTER!

THE YAK RULES AND YOU KNOW IT!

TOP 10 GOAL CELEBRATIONS!

MATCHFACTS! THE BEST NEWS & RESULTS!

FREE! FANTASY FOOTY GAME!

SEPT. 2-8 2008-09 SEASON £1.80

GBONLAHOR

YOUNG

N VILLA!

BAG YOU MEGA MAG EVERY TUESDAY!

THE HOTTEST STARS!

FANTASY FOOTY!

Pick a team of Premier League megastars and win top prizes!

MATCHFACTS!

Don't miss the best weekend results round-up in the world!

THE FA SKILLS!

Improve your skills every week with ace tips from top FA coaches!

TOUGH QUIZZES!

Prove you're a footy legend by tackling our awesome quizzes!

COOL POSTERS!

Plaster your bedroom wall with loads of wicked MATCH posters!

WICKED GEAR!

Check out all the latest footy gear and bag loads of world-class prizes!

LOG ON TO WWW.MATCHMAG.CO.UK

EXTRA-TIME! ★ IMPROVE YOUR GAME WITH THE FA SKILLS!

HOW TO...
HEAD THE BALL!

WORLD CUP ACTION!

England, Scotland, Wales, Northern Ireland and Ireland will be battling for a place at World Cup 2010! Don't miss all the awesome qualifying action!

CHAMPO LEAGUE!

MATCH can't get enough of the Champions League! Will another English club lift the famous trophy at Rome's Stadio Olimpico in May?

CLASS SKILLS TIPS!

Improve your game with the best coaches in the country! Read our FA Skills section every week then watch all the tips in action at matchmag.co.uk!

MATCH WEBSITE!

Check out all the latest footy news, play tons of top online games, watch flash movies, chat to MATCHMAN on the messageboards, and more!

WHAT'S GONNA ROCK IN 2009!

FANTASY FOOTY!

Did you miss our first game of the season? Then pick a team for Game 2 and you could win ace prizes! Check out MATCH mag to find out when it starts!

MATCH FANTASY FOOTY 2008-09!

MATCHFACTS!

Grab the best weekly results round-up for all four English divisions and the SPL! You'll love all the amazing stats!

THE ALL-NEW ADVENTURES OF **MATCHMAN**

MATCH TURNS 30!

Your fave footy mag will be a massive 30 years old in 2009! Keep reading MATCH to find out how we'll be celebrating!

ACE INTERVIEWS!

The biggest stars love chatting to MATCH! Read all the hottest interviews every week in the UK's best-selling footy mag!

MATCHMAN'S ADVENTURES!

MATCHY loves footy and knows loads of cool stars! Check out what he's been up to in his mega cartoon strip every week!

WE HOPE YOU ENJOYED THE MATCH ANNUAL 2009! SEE YOU NEXT YEAR!

THE UEFA CUP!

It was great watching Rangers power all the way to the final last season! We reckon it'll be just as good in 2008-09!